T0233298

Practical GraphQL

Learning Full-Stack GraphQL Development with Projects

Nabendu Biswas

Apress®

Practical GraphQL: Learning Full-Stack GraphQL Development with Projects

Nabendu Biswas
Bhopal, India

ISBN-13 (pbk): 978-1-4842-9620-2
https://doi.org/10.1007/978-1-4842-9621-9

ISBN-13 (electronic): 978-1-4842-9621-9

Managing Director, Apress Media LLC: Welmoed Spahr
Acquisitions Editor: James Robinson-Prior
Development Editor: James Markham
Editorial Assistant: Gryffin Winkler
Copyeditor: Kim Wimpsett

Cover designed by eStudioCalamar

Cover image designed by Freepik (www.freepik.com)

Distributed to the book trade worldwide by Springer Science+Business Media New York, 1 New York Plaza, Suite 4600, New York, NY 10004-1562, USA. Phone 1-800-SPRINGER, fax (201) 348-4505, e-mail orders-ny@springer-sbm.com, or visit www.springeronline.com. Apress Media, LLC is a California LLC and the sole member (owner) is Springer Science + Business Media Finance Inc (SSBM Finance Inc). SSBM Finance Inc is a **Delaware** corporation.

For information on translations, please e-mail booktranslations@springernature.com; for reprint, paperback, or audio rights, please e-mail bookpermissions@springernature.com.

Apress titles may be purchased in bulk for academic, corporate, or promotional use. eBook versions and licenses are also available for most titles. For more information, reference our Print and eBook Bulk Sales web page at http://www.apress.com/bulk-sales.

Any source code or other supplementary material referenced by the author in this book is available to readers on GitHub. For more detailed information, please visit https://www.apress.com/gp/services/source-code.

Paper in this product is recyclable

This book is affectionately dedicated to my wife and kid.

Table of Contents

About the Author

Nabendu Biswas is a full-stack JavaScript developer and has been working in the IT industry for the past 16 years for some of world's top development firms and investment banks. He is a passionate tech blogger and YouTuber and currently works as an Architect in an IT firm. He is also the author of six Apress books focusing on topics such as Gatsby, MERN, TypeScript and React Firebase, all of which can be found on Amazon.

About the Technical Reviewer

 **Preethi Vasudev** is an Oracle Certified Java programmer with more than 20 years of industry experience in investment banking, healthcare, and other domains. She has a master's degree from Auburn University, Alabama, and enjoys participating in coding competitions.

Introduction

GraphQL is revolutionizing how we develop and build websites. Seen as an alternative to REST APIs, this query language has become popular among developers and engineers who are looking for a query language to help them quickly develop and deploy applications and features with minimal fuss.

Starting with the basics, this book will teach you how to set up GraphQL and key details regarding queries and mutations, before moving on to more advanced, practical topics and projects.

You will gain a full understanding of the full web development ecosystem from front end to back end, by learning to build React applications using Prisma Apollo Client and MongoDB. Using a project-based approach, this book will equip you with all the practical knowledge needed to tackle full enterprise projects and turbocharge your skills and projects.

CHAPTER 1

Getting Started

In this book, you will learn about GraphQL. GraphQL is a new way to create APIs. Traditional APIs were created with REST. The problem with REST is that even when you need a subset of data, the endpoint gives all the data from the databases.

This is a waste of precious network resources. So, in this book, you will learn all about GraphQL. Here, you will learn to create APIs in a new way in NodeJS. You will also learn to connect them to the front end.

Initial Setup

In this first chapter, you will learn how to install GraphQL on your system. Also, you will learn to add extensions for GraphQL on VS Code to help you in the development process.

To start using GraphQL, you need to have NodeJS installed on your system. You will be using VS Code in your project. After that, you should also install an extension called GraphQL, which will be helpful in highlighting GraphQL in VS Code (Figure 1-1).

© Nabendu Biswas 2023

N. Biswas, *Practical GraphQL*, https://doi.org/10.1007/978-1-4842-9621-9_1

Figure 1-1. *GraphQL*

After that, create a folder named `ecomm-app-graphql` from the terminal. Inside it give the command `npm init -y` to create an empty node project. Next, give the following command to add `graphql` and `apollo- server` in the project:

```
1    npm i apollo-server graphql
```

There are different ways to use `graphql`, and `apollo` is the most popular one (Figure 1-2).

Figure 1-2. *npm install*

Summary

In this chapter, you installed the packages `apollo-server` and `graphql` in your system, through the terminal. You installed the official GraphQL extension in VS Code, which will help you in the development process. In the next chapter, you will learn about queries in GraphQL, which are similar to GET APIs in RESTful endpoints and are used to get the data from the database.

CHAPTER 2

Queries

In this chapter, we will start creating an e-commerce app and learn how to use GraphQL with it.

Setting Up the GraphQL Server

First, we will create an `index.js` file in our e-commerce app. Here, we import `ApolloServer` and `gql` first. With `gql`, we define the structure of the query. The query itself is given in resolvers.

After the resolvers, we create a server through an instance of `ApolloServer`, by passing `typeDefs` and `resolvers`. Lastly, we listen to this server on a predefined URL. See Listing 2-1.

Listing 2-1. index.js

```
const { ApolloServer, gql } = require("apollo-server");

const typeDefs = gql`
    type Query {
        welcome: String
    }
`
```

© Nabendu Biswas 2023
N. Biswas, *Practical GraphQL*, https://doi.org/10.1007/978-1-4842-9621-9_2

```
const resolvers = {
    Query: {
        welcome: () =>  {
            return "Weclome to the World of GraphQL"
        }
    }
}

const server = new ApolloServer({ typeDefs, resolvers })

server.listen().then(({ url}) => console.log(`Server is running
at ${url}`));
```

Run the command node index.js in the terminal; you will get the graphql server running on localhost:4000. Click the "Query your server" button.

The GraphQl playground (Figure 2-1) will open, and you will see the example query there.

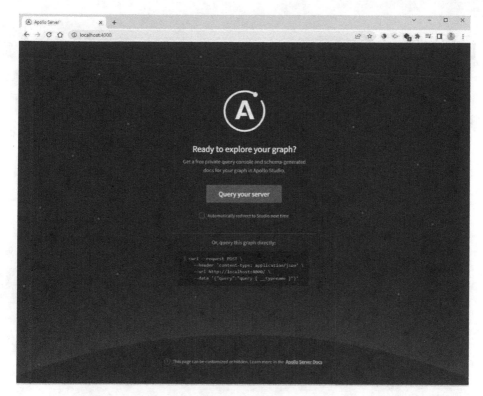

Figure 2-1. *Localhost*

Click the button ExampleQuery to get the result. See Figure 2-2.

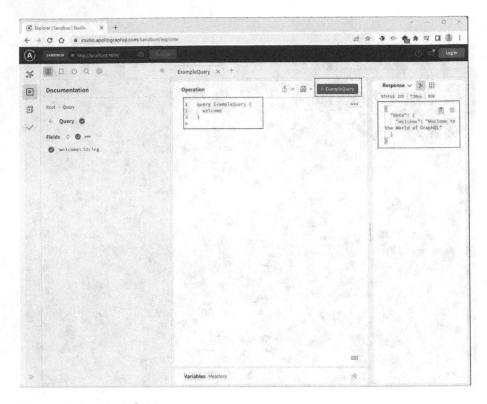

Figure 2-2. *GraphQL*

You don't want to make changes every time you update something in your code. For that reason, you will add nodemon in your project, using the command shown in Figure 2-3. Also update your script in the package. json file.

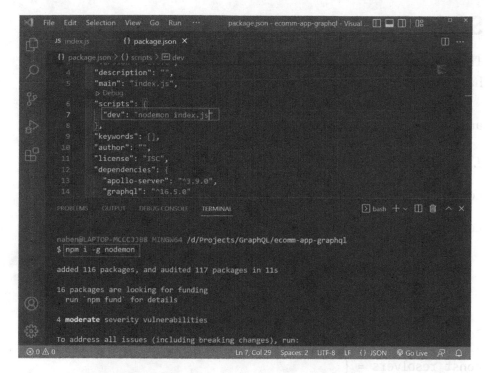

Figure 2-3. *Nodemon*

Next, run the command `npm run dev` from the project directory, and it will start the project with `nodemon`, as shown in Figure 2-4.

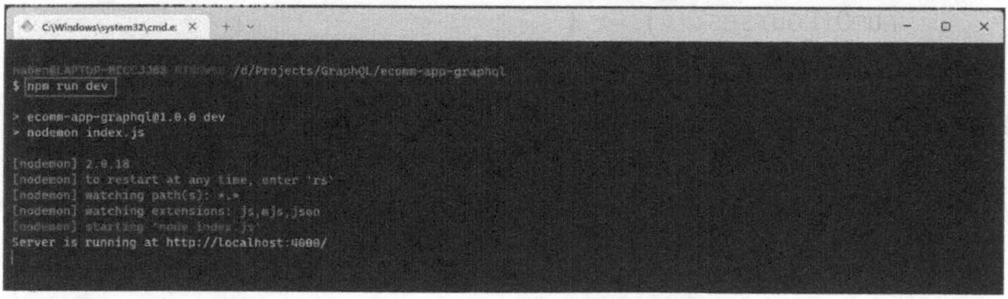

Figure 2-4. *npm run dev*

Scalar Types

There are four scalar types in GraphQL: String, Int, Float, and Boolean. We have already seen the String type in an earlier example.

Now, we will create an Int type in the query called numOfCourses. We are also returning it in the resolvers. See Listing 2-2.

Listing 2-2. Int Type

```
const { ApolloServer, gql } = require("apollo-server");

const typeDefs = gql`
    type Query {
        welcome: String
        numOfCourses: Int
    }
`

const resolvers = {
    Query: {
        welcome: () => {
            return "Weclome to the World of GraphQL"
        },
        numOfCourses: () => {
            return 12;
        }
    }
}
```

```
const server = new ApolloServer({ typeDefs, resolvers })
```

```
server.listen().then(({ url}) => console.log(`Server is running
at ${url}`));
```

```
server.listen().then(({ url}) => console.log(`Server is running
at ${url}`));
```

When running the query again in GraphQL, you will get the new data. See Figure 2-5.

Figure 2-5. *Int type*

Now, you will put in the rest of the types, which are Float and Boolean. We are defining them in both the query and the resolvers. See Listing 2-3.

Listing 2-3. All Types

```
const typeDefs = gql`
    type Query {
        welcome: String
        numOfCourses: Int
        price: Float
        isTrainer: Boolean
    }
`
```

```
const resolvers = {
    Query: {
        ...
        price: () => {
            return 1465.98;
        },
        isTrainer: () => {
            return true;
        }
    }
}
```

When running the query again in GraphQL, you will get all the new data back, as shown in Figure 2-6.

Figure 2-6. *All types*

In GraphQL, you can also pass null for any value; we are passing null for the String value, as shown in Listing 2-4.

Listing 2-4. Null Values

```
const typeDefs = gql`
    type Query {
        welcome: String
    ...
    }
`

const resolvers = {
    Query: {
        welcome: () =>  {
            return null
        },
    ...
    }
}
```

When running the query in GraphQL, you will get back null, as shown in Figure 2-7.

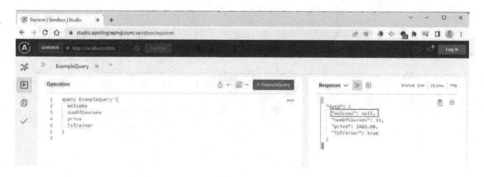

Figure 2-7. *GraphQL*

Since getting null is not desirable, you can add an ! in front of any Scalar type to specify that null is not allowed. See Listing 2-5.

Listing 2-5. Not Null

```
const typeDefs = gql`
    type Query {
        welcome: String!

        ...

    }
`

const resolvers = {
    Query: {
        welcome: () =>  {
            return null
        },
        ...
    }
}
```

Now, when you run the query, you will get an error, as shown in Figure 2-8.

Figure 2-8. *Error*

Array Types

In GraphQL we can have an array of all the Scalar types. In Listing 2-6, we have created a courses variable, which is an array of String. Now, we have to return an array of String in the resolvers.

Listing 2-6. Array of Strings

```
const typeDefs = gql`
    type Query {
        courses: [String]
        ...
    }

const resolvers = {
    Query: {
        courses: () =>  {
            return ['TypeScript', 'GraphQL', 'NextJS',
            'Angular']
            },
        ...
    }
}
```

When running the query in GraphQL, we will get back the array of strings, as shown in Figure 2-9.

Figure 2-9. *GraphQL*

Now, again the problem is that we can specify a null as a value in the array. Here, we will not get an error in GraphQL, as shown in Listing 2-7.

Listing 2-7. Null

```
const typeDefs = gql`
    type Query {
        courses: [String]
        ...
    }
`

const resolvers = {
    Query: {
        courses: () => {
            return ['TypeScript', null, 'NextJS', 'Angular']
            },
        ...
    }
}
```

We need to again add an ! in front of the String type for `null` to not be allowed. See Listing 2-8.

Listing 2-8. Null

```
const typeDefs = gql`
    type Query {
        courses: [String!]
        ...
    }

const resolvers = {
    Query: {
        courses: () => {
            return ['TypeScript', null, 'NextJS', 'Angular']
            },
        ...
    }
}
```

But still there is one problem. We can pass the whole array as a `null`, and we will not get an error. See Listing 2-9.

Listing 2-9. Null

```
const typeDefs = gql`
    type Query {
        courses: [String!]
        ...
    }
```

```
const resolvers = {
    Query: {
        courses: () => {
            return null
            },
        ...
    }
}
```

To solve this issue, we will add an ! in front of the array also. Now, we will get the desired error and not pass null for the array. See Listing 2-10.

Listing 2-10. Null Solved

```
const typeDefs = gql`
    type Query {
        courses: [String!]!
        ...
    }
`
const resolvers = {
    Query: {
        courses: () => {
            return null
            },
        ...
    }
}
```

Now, an array of string is accepted only for courses. See Listing 2-11.

Listing 2-11. Array of Strings

```
const typeDefs = gql`
    type Query {
        courses: [String!]!
        ...
    }
`

const resolvers = {
    Query: {
        courses: () => {
            return ['TypeScript', 'GraphQL', 'NextJS',
            'Angular']
            },
        ...
    }
}
```

Array of Objects

You will next learn how to show an array of objects in GraphQL. Here, we have created an array of objects called allCourses, which contains three objects. See Listing 2-12.

Listing 2-12. Array of Objects

```
const { ApolloServer, gql } = require("apollo-server");

const allCourses = [
    {
        name: "TypeScript Basics",
```

```
        description: "TypeScript Basics for beginners",
        price: 599.99,
        discount: false
    },
    {

        name: "GraphQL Basics",
        description: "GraphQL Basics for beginners",
        price: 499.99,
        discount: true

    },
    {

        name: "NextJS Basics",
        description: "NextJS Basics for beginners",
        price: 599.99,
        discount: false

    }
]
...
```

Now, in the typeDefs we will define a new type of Course, which will have some fields. This is an Object type, and we are using it in courses inside an array. We are also making the item and the array both mandatory.

Next, inside the resolvers we are passing allCourses. See Listing 2-13.

Listing 2-13. tyeDefs and Resolvers

```
const typeDefs = gql`
    type Query {
        courses: [Course!]!

        ...

    }
```

```
type Course {
    name: String!
    description: String!
    price: Float!
    discount: Boolean!
}


const resolvers = {
    Query: {
        courses: () => {
            return allCourses
        },
        ...
    }
}
```

Now, in the GraphQL sandbox, we can get the `courses` array of objects. See Figure 2-10.

Figure 2-10. *Sandbox*

Querying a Single Object

Now, you will learn to query a single object. Here, first we will update allCourses to courses and also add a unique ID to each object. See Listing 2-14.

Listing 2-14. courses

```
const courses = [
    {
        id: "book-06",
        name: "TypeScript Basics",
        description: "TypeScript Basics for beginners",
        price: 599.99,
        discount: false
    },
    {
        id: "book-07",
        name: "GraphQL Basics",
        description: "GraphQL Basics for beginners",
        price: 499.99,
        discount: true
    },
    {
        id: "book-08",
        name: "NextJS Basics",
        description: "NextJS Basics for beginners",
        price: 599.99,
        discount: false
    }
]
```

Next, we will create a type of course, in which we need to pass the ID. Here, again we are referencing the Course object.

We have also updated courses in our resolvers to return the courses. Beside this we have a course resolver, which will take the ID from the args. After that, it will find the course with the ID and return it. See Listing 2-15.

Listing 2-15. Resolvers

```
const typeDefs = gql`
    type Query {
        courses: [Course!]!
        course(id: ID!): Course
        numOfCourses: Int
        ...
    }


const resolvers = {
    Query: {
        courses: () =>  courses,
        course: (parent, args, context) => {
            const courseId = args.id;
            const course = courses.find(item => item.id ===
            courseId);
            if(!course) return null;
            else return course;
        },
```

Now, when we query a particular book in the Apollo Sandbox, we will get the course. See Figure 2-11.

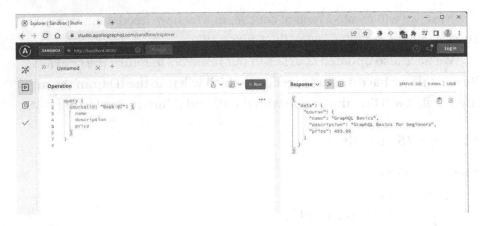

Figure 2-11. *Sandbox*

Queries for Genres

Now, we will create a new query for genres. Here, we will have two objects
containing two genres within an array.

Next, we have genres and genre in typeDefs and the object for it.
Notice that it is quite similar to courses. See Listing 2-16.

Listing 2-16. genres

```
const genres = [
    { id: 'cat-01', name: 'Technical' },
    { id: 'cat-02', name: 'History' }
]

const typeDefs = gql`
    type Query {
        courses: [Course!]!
        course(id: ID!): Course
        genres: [Genre!]!
        genre(id: ID!): Genre
```

```
        numOfCourses: Int
        price: Float
        isTrainer: Boolean
    }

    type Genre{
        id: ID!
        name: String!
    }
```

Next, we will have the resolvers for genres and genre. Again, it is quite similar to what we have for courses. See Listing 2-17.

Listing 2-17. Resolvers

```
const resolvers = {
    Query: {
        courses: () =>  courses,
        course: (parent, args, context) => {
            const courseId = args.id;
            const course = courses.find(item => item.id ===
            courseId);
            if(!course) return null;
            else return course;
        },
        genres: () => genres,
        genre: (parent, args, context) => {
            const catId = args.id;
            const genre = genres.find(item => item.id
            === catId);
            if(!genre) return null;
```

```
            else return genre;
        },
        ...
    }
}
```

Now, when we query for a particular genre in the Apollo Sandbox, we will get the data for it back. See Figure 2-12.

Figure 2-12. *Sandbox*

Also, the query for all genres gives us the desired result. See Figure 2-13.

Figure 2-13. *Sandbox*

Relating Genre to Courses

To relate a particular genre to courses, we need to first add a genreId to all courses. See Listing 2-18.

Listing 2-18. Courses

```
const courses = [
    ...
    {
        id: "book-08",
        name: "NextJS Basics",
        description: "NextJS Basics for beginners",
        price: 599.99,
        discount: false,
        genreId: "cat-01"
    },
```

```
    {
        id: "book-21",
        name: "The Immortals of Meluha",
        description: "Shiva Trilogy -1",
        price: 299.99,
        discount: false,
        genreId: "cat-02"
    },
    {
        id: "book-22",
        name: "The Secret of the Nagas",
        description: "Shiva Trilogy -2",
        price: 199.99,
        discount: true,
        genreId: "cat-02"
    },
    {
        id: "book-23",
        name: "The Oath of the Vayuputras",
        description: "Shiva Trilogy -3",
        price: 599.99,
        discount: false,
        genreId: "cat-02"
    }
]
```

Next, in the object for Genre in the typeDef, we will add courses. It will be an array with a mandatory item and array.

Then, in the resolver, we need to add a new item of Genre. Here, in courses, we are first getting the genreId from the parent. After that, we are filtering based on it to get back the filtered courses. See Listing 2-19.

Listing 2-19. Resolvers

```
const typeDefs = gql`
    ...
    type Genre{
        id: ID!
        name: String!
        courses: [Course!]!
    }
`

 const resolvers = {
    Query: {
    ...
    },
    Genre: {
        courses: (parent, args, context) => {
            const genreId = parent.id;
            return courses.filter(item => item.genreId ===
            genreId);
        }
    }
}
```

Now, we can query a genre with a particular ID and get the courses in it. See Figure 2-14.

Figure 2-14. *Genres*

Relating Courses to Genre

To relate a genre to Course, we need to add it in the type for Course first. After that, in the resolvers, we will make a new item for Course. Here, from the genre we are getting the genreId from the parent, which is Course. See Listing 2-20.

Listing 2-20. genre

```
const typeDefs = gql`
    type Course {
        id: ID!
        name: String!
        description: String!
        price: Float!
        discount: Boolean!
        genre: Genre
    }


 const resolvers = {
    Query: {
        ...
    },
    Genre: {
        ...
    }
    Course: {
        genre: (parent, args, context) => {
            const genreId = parent.genreId;
                return genres.find(item => item.id ===
                genreId);
        }
    }
}
```

Next, our courses will also provide the genre when we run it from the Apollo Sandbox. See Figure 2-15.

Figure 2-15. *Genre*

Reorganizing the Code

Now, we will reorganize our code, because we have a giant `index.js` file. The first thing that we will do is create a `schema.js` file in the root directory. Here, we are importing `gql` first and then exporting `typeDefs`. We have cut this code from the `index.js` file. See Listing 2-21.

Listing 2-21. schema.js

```
const { gql } = require("apollo-server");

exports.typeDefs = gql`
    type Query {
        courses: [Course!]!
        course(id: ID!): Course
        genres: [Genre!]!
        genre(id: ID!): Genre
```

```
    numOfCourses: Int
    price: Float
    isTrainer: Boolean
}

type Course {
    id: ID!
    name: String!
    description: String!
    price: Float!
    discount: Boolean!
    genre: Genre
}
type Genre{
    id: ID!
    name: String!
    courses: [Course!]!
}
```

Next, in the index.js file, we will import typeDefs. We have already deleted it from Listing 2-22.

Listing 2-22. index.js

```
const { ApolloServer } = require("apollo-server");
const { typeDefs } = require("./schema");
```

Next, the courses and genres will go to a file called database.js from the index.js file. We are also exporting them from here. See Listing 2-23.

Listing 2-23. database.js

```
const courses = [
    ...
]
const genres = [
    { id: 'cat-01', name: 'Technical' },
    { id: 'cat-02', name: 'History' }
]
module.exports = { courses, genres }
```

Now, we will use them in the index.js file. See Listing 2-24.

Listing 2-24. index.js

```
const { ApolloServer } = require("apollo-server");
const { typeDefs } = require("./schema");
const { courses, genres } = require("./database");
```

Next, create a resolvers folder in the root directory and create a file called Query.js inside it. Here, we are importing courses and genres from the database file and exporting the query, which we have taken from the index.js file. See Listing 2-25.

Listing 2-25. Query.js

```
const { courses, genres } = require("../database");

exports.Query = {
    courses: () =>  courses,
    ...
}
```

Now, create a `Course.js` file inside the `resolvers` folder. Here, add the Course resolver from the `index.js` file. See Listing 2-26.

Listing 2-26. Course.js

```
const { genres } = require("../database");

exports.Course = {
    genre: (parent, args, context) => {
        const genreId = parent.genreId;
        return genres.find(item => item.id === genreId);
    }
}
```

Now, create a `Genre.js` file inside the `resolvers` folder. Here, add the Course resolver from the `index.js` file. See Listing 2-27.

Listing 2-27. Genre.js

```
const { courses } = require("../database");

exports.Genre ={
    courses: (parent, args, context) => {
        const genreId = parent.id;
        return courses.filter(item => item.genreId ===
        genreId);
    }
}
```

Finally, add these in the `index.js` file. Our `index.js` file is finally the starting point, and all the code is transferred to small manageable files. See Listing 2-28.

Listing 2-28. index.js

```
const { ApolloServer } = require("apollo-server");
const { typeDefs } = require("./schema");
const { Query } = require("./resolvers/Query");
const { Course } = require("./resolvers/Course");
const { Genre } = require("./resolvers/Genre");

const server = new ApolloServer({ typeDefs, resolvers: { Query,
Course, Genre }})

server.listen().then(({ url}) => console.log(`Server is running
at ${url}`));
```

Using Context

We are importing the database in all of our resolvers. Instead of this, we can use the context parameter. So, first import courses and genres from the database in the index.js file. Then we will add this in the instance of Apollo Server. See Listing 2-29.

Listing 2-29. index.js

```
const { courses, genres } = require("./database");
const server = new ApolloServer({ typeDefs, resolvers: { Query,
Course, Genre }, context: { courses, genres }})
```

Now, we will delete the import of the database from the Course.js file. We will use the context to get the genres here. See Listing 2-30.

Listing 2-30. Course.js

```
exports.Course = {
    genre: (parent, args, context) => {
            const genres = context.genres;
            const genreId = parent.genreId;
            return genres.find(item => item.id === genreId);
    }
}
```

Similarly, we will delete the import of the database from the Genre.js file. We will use the context to get the courses here. See Listing 2-31.

Listing 2-31. Genre.js

```
exports.Genre ={
    courses: (parent, args, context) => {
        const courses = context.courses;
        const genreId = parent.id;
        return courses.filter(item => item.genreId ===
        genreId);
    }
}
```

In the Query.js file, we will use both courses and genres. See Listing 2-32.

Listing 2-32. Query.js

```
exports.Query = {
    courses: (parent, args, context) =>  {
        const courses = context.courses;
        return courses;
    },
```

```
    course: (parent, args, context) => {
        const courseId = args.id;
        const courses = context.courses;
        const course = courses.find(item => item.id ===
        courseId);
        if(!course) return null;
        else return course;
    },
    genres: (parent, args, context) => {
        const genres = context.genres;
        return genres;
    },
    genre: (parent, args, context) => {
        const catId = args.id;
        const genres = context.genres;
        const genre = genres.find(item => item.id === catId);
        if(!genre) return null;
        else return genre;
    },
    ...
}
```

Now, when we run a query, we get the correct result. It means
everything is working fine. See Figure 2-16.

Figure 2-16. *Sandbox*

Adding Reviews

We will add the capability of reviews in our project. First, we will add an array of objects in the database.js file. Here, the courseId is the id of each course. See Listing 2-33.

Listing 2-33. database.js

```
const reviews = [
    {
        id: "rev-01",
        date: "2021-01-01",
        title: "This is bad",
        comment: "when i bought this it broke the computer",
        rating: 1,
        courseId: "book-06",
    },
```

```
    ...
];
module.exports = { courses, genres, reviews }
```

Next, we will import and use it in the index.js file. See Listing 2-34.

Listing 2-34. index.js

```
const { courses, genres, reviews } = require("./database");

const server = new ApolloServer({
    typeDefs,
    resolvers: { Query, Course, Genre },
    context: { courses, genres, reviews }
})
```

Now in the schema.js file, in the type of the Course we will add reviews, which will be an array of objects. We are also adding a type for Review. See Listing 2-35.

Listing 2-35. schema.js

```
exports.typeDefs = gql`
    ...
    type Course {
        id: ID!
        name: String!
        description: String!
        price: Float!
        discount: Boolean!
        genre: Genre
        reviews: [Review!]!
    }
```

```
type Genre{
    id: ID!
    name: String!
    courses: [Course!]!
}
type Review {
    id: ID!
    date: String!
    title: String!
    comment: String!
    rating: Int!
}
```

Next, inside the Course.js file, we will add the function for reviews. Here, for each review, we are checking whether it belongs to a course. See Listing 2-36.

Listing 2-36. Course.js

```
exports.Course = {
    genre: (parent, args, context) => {
        ...
    },
    reviews: (parent, args, context) => {
        const reviews = context.reviews;
        const { id } = parent;
        return reviews.filter(item => item.courseId === id);

    }
}
```

Now, for a particular course, we can get the reviews also. See Figure 2-17.

Figure 2-17. *Studio*

Adding Filtering

Now, we will add filtering logic in our GraphQL queries. First in the
schema.js file, we will add a filter in the courses. This is an input type, so
we have to create it separately. We will have the filter on the discount. See
Listing 2-37.

Listing 2-37. Schema.js

```
exports.typeDefs = gql`
    type Query {
        courses(filter: CoursesFilter): [Course!]!
        course(id: ID!): Course
        genres: [Genre!]!
        genre(id: ID!): Genre
        numOfCourses: Int
        price: Float
        isTrainer: Boolean
    }
```

```
input CoursesFilter {
    discount: Boolean
}
...
```

Now, in the `Query.js` file, we will update the `courses`. Here, we are getting the `filter` from the args. Then we are checking if the discount is there, and we are filtering courses on it. See Listing 2-38.

Listing 2-38. Query.js

```
exports.Query = {
    courses: (parent, args, context) => {
        let filteredCourses = context.courses;
        const { filter } = args;
        if(filter) {
            if(filter.discount){
                filteredCourses = filteredCourses.filter
                (product => product.discount);
            }
        }
        return filteredCourses;
    },
    ...
}
```

Now, we can check the courses that have a discount in the sandbox. See Figure 2-18.

Figure 2-18. *Studio*

Again, in the schema.js file, we will add a filter in the Genre for courses. See Listing 2-39.

Listing 2-39. Schema.js

```
exports.typeDefs = gql`
    type Query {
        input CoursesFilter {
        discount: Boolean
    }
    type Genre{
        id: ID!
        name: String!
        courses(filter: CoursesFilter): [Course!]!
    }
`
```

Now, in the Genre.js file, we will update the courses. Here, we are first getting the filter from the args. Then we are checking if the discount is there, and we are filtering courses on it. See Listing 2-40.

Listing 2-40. Genre.js

```
exports.Genre ={
    courses: (parent, args, context) => {
        const courses = context.courses;
        const genreId = parent.id;
        const { filter } = args;
        const genreProducts = courses.filter(item => item.
        genreId === genreId);
        let filteredGenre = genreProducts;
        if(filter){
            if(filter.discount){
                filteredGenre = filteredGenre.filter(product =>
                product.discount);
            }
        }
        return filteredGenre;
    }
}
```

Now, for each genre, we can get the discounted courses. See Figure 2-19.

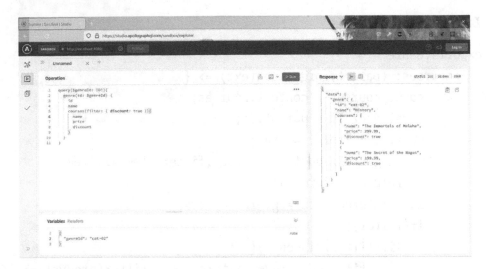

Figure 2-19. *Studio*

Filter by Average Rating

Now, we will add the logic in GraphQL where a user can get reviews greater than the average ratings. For this in the `schema.js` file in the `CoursesFilter`, we will add an `avgRating` variable of type Int. See Listing 2-41.

Listing 2-41. schema.js

```
exports.typeDefs = gql`
    input CoursesFilter {
        discount: Boolean
        avgRating: Int
    }
`
```

Now, we will update the logic for the filter in the Query.js file. Here, we are checking whether avgRating is in the rating of 1, 2, 3, 4, 5. Next, for each review we are getting the average. See Listing 2-42.

Listing 2-42. Query.js

```
exports.Query = {
    courses: (parent, args, context) =>  {
        let filteredCourses = context.courses;
        const { filter } = args;
        let { reviews } = context;
        if(filter){
            const { discount, avgRating } = filter;
            if(discount) filteredCourses = filteredCourses.
            filter(product => product.discount);
            if([1, 2, 3, 4, 5].includes(avgRating)){
                filteredCourses = filteredCourses.
                filter(item => {
                    let sum = 0;
                    let numOfReviews = 0;
                    reviews.forEach((review) => {
                        if(review.courseId === item.id){
                            sum += review.rating;
                            numOfReviews++;
                        }
                    })
                    const avgCourseRating = sum / numOfReviews;
                    return avgCourseRating >= avgRating;
                })
            }
        }
```

```
        return filteredCourses;
    },
    ...
}
```

Now, when we pass the `avgRating` in courses, we will have only the ratings associated with it. See Figure 2-20.

Figure 2-20. *Studio*

Summary

In this chapter, we set up the GraphQL server. After that, you learned about different types such as scalars and arrays. Next, you learned to query through GraphQL, which is like the GET API in RESTful endpoints.

In the next chapter, you will learn about mutations in GraphQL, which are similar to POST APIs in RESTful endpoints and are used to store data in the database.

CHAPTER 3

Mutations

In this chapter, you will learn about mutations. With mutations, you basically create, update, and delete your data. It is like the POST, PUT, and DELETE operations of the RESTful API.

Creating Data

You need to add a mutation in the schema.js file first. Here, we will create a new type of mutation. Inside it we will create our first mutation of addGenre, which will take input and also return the genre. See Listing 3-1.

Listing 3-1. schema.js

```
exports.typeDefs = gql`
    type Query {
        courses(filter: CoursesFilter): [Course!]!
        course(id: ID!): Course
        genres: [Genre!]!
        genre(id: ID!): Genre
        numOfCourses: Int
        price: Float
        isTrainer: Boolean
    }
```

© Nabendu Biswas 2023
N. Biswas, *Practical GraphQL*, https://doi.org/10.1007/978-1-4842-9621-9_3

```
type Mutation {
    addGenre(input: AddGenreInput!): Genre!
}
input AddGenreInput {
    name: String!
}
```
`

Next, we will create a new file named Mutation.js. Here, we are first importing the UUID, which we need to install by using npm i uuid.

In the Mutation.js file, we are adding the addGenre, which will again take the parameters of the parent, args and context. We are getting the name from args and the genres from context.

After that, we create a new genre from the UUI and name and then push it to the array of genres. See Listing 3-2.

Listing 3-2. Mutation.js

```
const { v4: uuid } = require("uuid");

exports.Mutation = {
    addGenre: (parent, args, context) => {
        const { input } = args;
        const { name } = input;
        const { genres } = context;

        const newGene = { id: uuid(), name }
        genres.push(newGene)
        return newGene
    }
}
```

Now, we need to add this mutation to our resolvers in the index.js file. See Listing 3-3.

Listing 3-3. index.js

```
const { typeDefs } = require("./schema");
const { Mutation } = require("./resolvers/Mutation");
const { Query } = require("./resolvers/Query");

const server = new ApolloServer({
    typeDefs,
    resolvers: { Query, Mutation, Course, Genre },
    context: { courses, genres, reviews }
})
```

To check the mutation, we need to give the GraphQL query of the mutation and pass the input. It will add a new genre and return the unique ID, as shown in Figure 3-1.

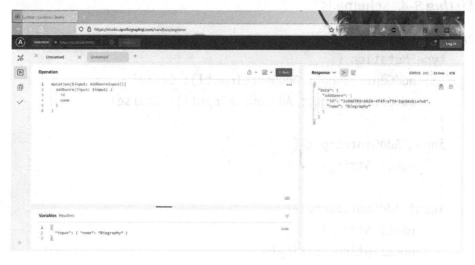

Figure 3-1. *Apollo*

Now, when we check the **genres**, we will get the new genre. See Figure 3-2.

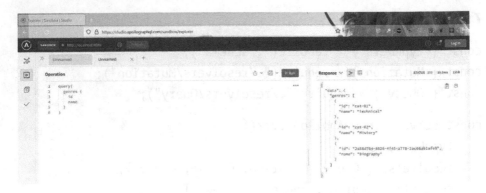

Figure 3-2. *Apollo query*

Similarly, we will add the mutation for addCourse in the schema.js file.
See Listing 3-4.

Listing 3-4. schema.js

```
exports.typeDefs = gql`
    type Mutation {
        addGenre(input: AddGenreInput!): Genre!
        addCourse(input: AddCourseInput!): Course!
    }
    input AddGenreInput {
        name: String!
    }
    input AddCourseInput{
        name: String!
        description: String!
        price: Float!
        discount: Boolean!
        genreId: ID!
    }
`
```

Similarly, we will add the addCourse function in the file Muta- tion. js. See Listing 3-5.

Listing 3-5. Mutation.js

```
exports.Mutation = {
    addCourse: (parent, args, context) => {
        const { input } = args;
        const { name, description, price, discount,
        genreId } = input;
        const { courses } = context;

        const newCourse = { id: uuid(), name, description,
        price, discount, genreId }
        courses.push(newCourse)
        return newCourse
    }
}
```

To check the mutation, we need to give the GraphQL query of the mutation and pass the input. This will add a new course and return the unique ID. See Figure 3-3.

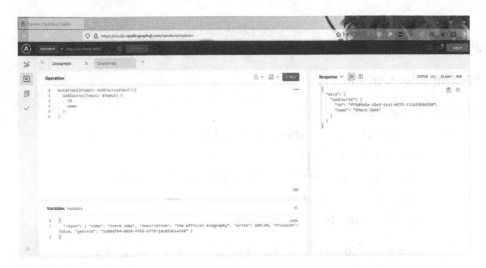

Figure 3-3. *Apollo*

Now, when we check the `courses`, we will get the new course. See Figure 3-4.

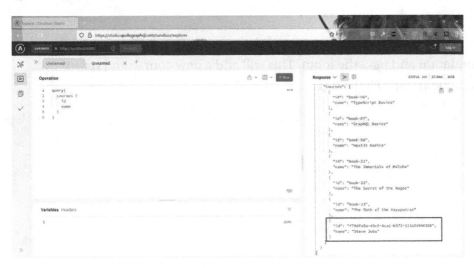

Figure 3-4. *Apollo query*

The mutation for addReview in the schema.js file will also be similar. See Listing 3-6.

Listing 3-6. Schema.jss

```
exports.typeDefs = gql`
    type Mutation {
        addGenre(input: AddGenreInput!): Genre!
        addCourse(input: AddCourseInput!): Course!
        addReview(input: AddReviewInput!): Review!
    }
    input AddReviewInput {
        date: String!
        title: String!
        comment: String!
        rating: Int!
        courseId: ID!
    }
```

Again, we will add the addReview function in the file Mutation.js. See Listing 3-7.

Listing 3-7. Mutation.js

```
exports.Mutation = {
    addReview: (parent, args, context) => {
        const { input } = args;
        const { date, title, comment, rating, courseId }
        = input;
        const { reviews } = context;
        const newReview = { id: uuid(), date, title, comment,
        rating, courseId }
```

```
        reviews.push(newReview)
        return newReview
    },
}
```

To check the mutation, we need to give the GraphQL query of the mutation and pass the input. This will add a new review and return the unique ID. See Figure 3-5.

Figure 3-5. *Apollo*

Now, when we check the courses, we will get the new review. See Figure 3-6.

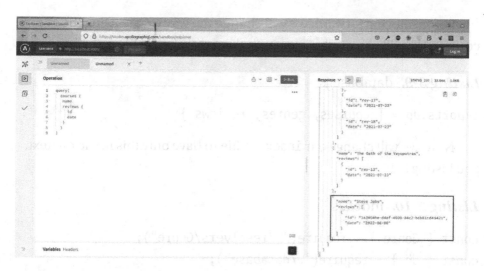

Figure 3-6. *Apollo query*

Deleting Data

We will now write the mutation to delete data in the schema.js file. Here, we will create a mutation of deleteGenre. We just need to pass the ID, and we will get back a Boolean. See Listing 3-8.

Listing 3-8. schema.js

```
exports.typeDefs = gql`
    type Mutation {
        addGenre(input: AddGenreInput!): Genre!
        addCourse(input: AddCourseInput!): Course!
        addReview(input: AddReviewInput!): Review!
        deleteGenre(id: ID!): Boolean!
    }
```

Before moving forward, we will change the way we are using the context. We will change the exports in the database.js file. See Listing 3-9.

Listing 3-9. database.js

```
exports.db = { courses, genres, reviews }
```

Now, we will change our index.js file to have only this in the context. See Listing 3-10.

Listing 3-10. index.js

```
const { Genre } = require("./resolvers/Genre");
const { db } = require("./database");

const server = new ApolloServer({
    typeDefs,
    resolvers: { Query, Mutation, Course, Genre },
    context: { db }
})
```

So, now we will get the db from the context. We will change it first in the Course.js file. See Listing 3-11.

Listing 3-11. Course.js

```
exports.Course = {
    genre: (parent, args, context) => {
        const db = context.db;
        const genreId = parent.genreId;
        return db.genres.find(item => item.id === genreId);
    },
    reviews: (parent, args, context) => {
        const db = context.db;
        const { id } = parent;
```

```
    return db.reviews.filter(item => item.courseId === id);
  }
}
```

Next, we will change it in the Genre.js file. See Listing 3-12.

Listing 3-12. Genre.js

```
exports.Genre ={
    courses: (parent, args, context) => {
        const { db } = context;
        const genreId = parent.id;
        const { filter } = args;
        const genreProducts = db.courses.filter(item => item.
        genreId === genreId);
        let filteredGenre = genreProducts;
        ...
        return filteredGenre;
    }
}
```

Next, we will change it in the Query.js file for courses.

We will also change the other part in the Query.js file. See Listing 3-13.

Listing 3-13. Query.js

```
exports.Query = {
    courses: (parent, args, { db }) => {
        let filteredCourses = db.courses;
        const { filter } = args;
        if(filter){
            const { discount, avgRating } = filter;
            if(discount) filteredCourses = filteredCourses.
            filter(product => product.discount);
```

```
        if([1, 2, 3, 4, 5].includes(avgRating)){
            filteredCourses = filteredCourses.
            filter(item => {
                let sum = 0;
                let numOfReviews = 0;
                db.reviews.forEach((review) => {
        ...
                })
                const avgCourseRating = sum / numOfReviews;
                return avgCourseRating >= avgRating;
            })
        }
    }
    return filteredCourses;
},
course: (parent, args, { db }) => {
    const courseId = args.id;
    const course = db.courses.find(item => item.id ===
    courseId);
    if(!course) return null;
    else return course;
},
genres: (parent, args, { db }) => db.generes,
genre: (parent, args, { db }) => {
    const catId = args.id;
    const genre = db.genres.find(item => item.id
    === catId);
    if(!genre) return null;
    else return genre;
},
...
}
```

Similarly, we will change it in the `Mutation.js` file. See Listing 3-14.

Listing 3-14. Mutation.js

```
exports.Mutation = {
    addGenre: (parent, args, { db }) => {
        const { input } = args;
        const { name } = input;
        const newGene = { id: uuid(), name }
        db.genres.push(newGene)
        return newGene
    },
    addCourse: (parent, args, { db }) => {
        const { input } = args;
        const { name, description, price, discount, genreId }
        = input;
        const newCourse = { id: uuid(), name, description,
        price, discount, genreId }
        db.courses.push(newCourse)
        return newCourse
    },
    addReview: (parent, args, { db }) => {
        const { input } = args;
        const { date, title, comment, rating, courseId }
        = input;
        const newReview = { id: uuid(), date, title, comment,
        rating, courseId }
        db.reviews.push(newReview)
        return newReview
    },
}
```

Finally, we will create the function for deleteGenre in the Mutation.js file. Here, we are first filtering out the passed genre from the genres array.

Now, each genre has multiple courses associated with it. We are just making the genreId value null in it so that we can use it at a later point. See Listing 3-15.

Listing 3-15. Mutation.js

```
exports.Mutation = {
    deleteGenre: (parent, { id }, { db }) => {
        db.genres = db.genres.filter(genre => genre.id !== id);
        db.courses = db.courses.map(course => {
            if(course.genreId === id){
                return {...course, genreId: null}
            } else {
                return course
            }
        })
        return true;
    }
}
```

Next, in the Studio we will run the deleteGenre mutation with a ID, and we will get back true. See Figure 3-7.

Figure 3-7. *Apollo*

Now, when we see the courses for this genre, we will get the genre as null. See Figure 3-8.

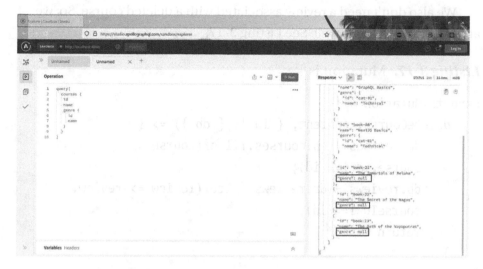

Figure 3-8. *Apollo*

Next, we will add the mutation of deleteCourse in the schema.js file. We just need to pass the ID, and we will get back a Boolean. See Listing 3-16.

Listing 3-16. schema.js

```
exports.typeDefs = gql`
    type Mutation {
        addGenre(input: AddGenreInput!): Genre!
        addCourse(input: AddCourseInput!): Course!
        addReview(input: AddReviewInput!): Review!
        deleteGenre(id: ID!): Boolean!
        deleteCourse(id: ID!): Boolean!
    }
`
```

We will create the function for deleteCourse in the Mutation.js file. Here, we are first filtering out the passed course from the courses array.

We also don't need a review associated with a deleted course. So, we are filtering out that as well. See Listing 3-17.

Listing 3-17. Mutation.js

```
exports.Mutation = {
    deleteCourse: (parent, { id }, { db }) => {
        db.courses = db.courses.filter(course =>
        course.id !== id);
        db.reviews = db.reviews.filter(review => review.
        courseId !== id);
        return true;
    }
}
```

Now, in Studio we will see all the courses with reviews. See Figure 3-9.

Figure 3-9. *Apollo*

We will delete the course, which we saw earlier by passing its ID in the mutation of `deleteCourse`. See Figure 3-10.

Figure 3-10. *Apollo*

Now, again when we query all the courses, the course with the ID `book-06` is gone, along with its reviews. See Figure 3-11.

Figure 3-11. *Apollo*

Lastly, we will add the mutation of `deleteReview` in the `schema.js` file. We just need to pass the ID, and we will get back a Boolean. See Listing 3-18.

Listing 3-18. schema.js

```
type Mutation {
    addGenre(input: AddGenreInput!): Genre!
    addCourse(input: AddCourseInput!): Course!
    addReview(input: AddReviewInput!): Review!
    deleteGenre(id: ID!): Boolean!
    deleteCourse(id: ID!): Boolean!
    deleteReview(id: ID!): Boolean!
}
```

We will create the function for deleteReview in the Mutation.js file. Here, we are filtering out the passed review from the reviews array. See Listing 3-19.

Listing 3-19. Mutation.js

```
exports.Mutation = {
    deleteReview: (parent, { id }, { db }) => {
        db.reviews = db.reviews.filter(review => review.id
        !== id);
        return true;
    }
}
```

Now, in Studio we will see all the courses with reviews. See Figure 3-12.

66

Figure 3-12. *Apollo*

We will delete one particular review, which we saw earlier by passing its ID in the mutation of `deleteReview`. See Figure 3-13.

Figure 3-13. *Apollo*

Now, again when we query all the courses, the review with ID `rev-01` is gone. See Figure 3-14.

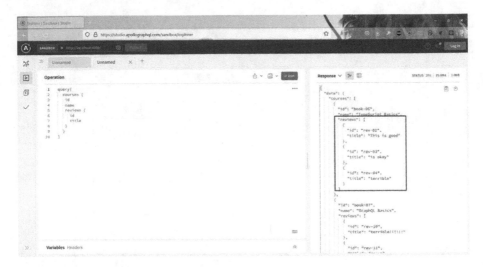

Figure 3-14. *Apollo*

Updating Data

We will write the mutations to update the existing data next. So, first we
will create a mutation of updateGenre in the schema.js file. We just need
to pass the ID and the input type here. See Listing 3-20.

Listing 3-20. schema.js

```
exports.typeDefs = gql`
    type Mutation {
        addGenre(input: AddGenreInput!): Genre!
        addCourse(input: AddCourseInput!): Course!
        addReview(input: AddReviewInput!): Review!
        deleteGenre(id: ID!): Boolean!
        deleteCourse(id: ID!): Boolean!
        deleteReview(id: ID!): Boolean!
        updateGenre(id: ID!, input: UpdateGenreInput!): Genre!
    }
```

```
input UpdateGenreInput {
    name: String!
}
```

We will create the function for updateGenre in the Mutation.js file.
Here, we are first finding the particular genre from the ID. After that, we are
using the spread operator to spread all the data of the particular genre and
the passed input. If any field will be updated, it will be replaced, as objects
cannot have duplicate keys. See Listing 3-21.

Listing 3-21. Mutation.js

```
exports.Mutation = {
    updateGenre: (parent, { id, input }, { db }) => {
        const index = db.genres.findIndex(genre => genre.id
        === id);
        db.genres[index] = {...db.genres[index], ...input};
        return db.genres[index];
    },
}
```

Now, we will query all the genres in Studio. See Figure 3-15.

Figure 3-15. *Apollo*

Next, we will pass the ID and the updated name in the mutation of updateGenre in Studio, and it will be updated successfully. See Figure 3-16.

Figure 3-16. *Apollo*

Again, we will query all the genres in Studio. And our genre is updated properly. See Figure 3-17.

Figure 3-17. *Apollo*

Next, we will add the definitions of updateCourse and updateReview in the schema.js file. Also, notice that the return value is optional now and we have removed the !. See Listing 3-22.

Listing 3-22. schema.js

```
type Mutation {
    addGenre(input: AddGenreInput!): Genre!
    addCourse(input: AddCourseInput!): Course!
    addReview(input: AddReviewInput!): Review!
    deleteGenre(id: ID!): Boolean!
    deleteCourse(id: ID!): Boolean!
    deleteReview(id: ID!): Boolean!
    updateGenre(id: ID!, input: UpdateGenreInput!): Genre
    updateCourse(id: ID!, input:
    UpdateCourseInput!): Course
    updateReview(id: ID!, input:
    UpdateReviewInput!): Review
}
```

Now, further in the schema.js file, we will add the input for updateCourse. Also, notice that genreId is not mandatory. See Listing 3-23.

Listing 3-23. schema.js

```
input AddCourseInput{
    name: String!
    description: String!
    price: Float!
    discount: Boolean!
    genreId: ID
}
input UpdateCourseInput {
    name: String!
    description: String!
    price: Float!
```

```
    discount: Boolean!
    genreId: ID
}
```

Next, we will also add the input for updateReview in the schema.js file. See Listing 3-24.

Listing 3-24. schema.js

```
input UpdateReviewInput {
    date: String!
    title: String!
    comment: String!
    rating: Int!
    courseId: ID!
}
```

Now, in the Mutation.js file, we will add the functions updateCourse and updateReview. They are similar to the function updateGenre. Also, notice that we can receive the wrong input now and return a null. See Listing 3-25.

Listing 3-25. Mutation.js

```
exports.Mutation = {
    updateGenre: (parent, { id, input }, { db }) => {
        const index = db.genres.findIndex(genre =>
        genre.id === id);
        if(index === -1) return null
        db.genres[index] = {...db.genres[index], ...input};
        return db.genres[index];
    },
    updateCourse: (parent, { id, input }, { db }) => {
```

```
        const index = db.courses.findIndex(course =>
        course.id === id);
        if(index === -1) return null
        db.courses[index] = {...db.courses[index], ...input};
        return db.courses[index];
    },
    updateReview: (parent, { id, input }, { db }) => {
        const index = db.reviews.findIndex(review =>
        review.id === id);
        if(index === -1) return null
        db.reviews[index] = {...db.reviews[index], ...input};
        return db.reviews[index];
    }

}
```

Now, we will check all the courses in Sandbox. See Figure 3-18.

Figure 3-18. *Apollo*

Next, we will update a course by passing all the fields in the mutation. Notice that we have changed the price and discount only. See Figure 3-19.

Figure 3-19. *Apollo*

Back in the query, the two fields are updated. See Figure 3-20.

Figure 3-20. *Apollo*

Summary

In this chapter, you learned about mutations in GraphQL. You learned to create data, delete data, and update data.

In the next chapter, we will create a new app. Here, you will learn to create a full-stack app with GraphQL.

CHAPTER 4

Full-Stack GraphQL

In this chapter, we will build a full-stack app with GraphQL and React. We will use Apollo for the back end and then the Apollo client to connect from the front end.

The Setup

We will first create a new folder called graphql-project-mgmt and then inside it create a folder named server. Now, inside the server folder, we will create an empty package.json file by giving the command npm init -y. See Listing 4-1.

Listing 4-1. The Setup

```
mkdir graphql-project-mgmt
cd graphql-project-mgmt
mkdir server
cd server
npm init -y
```

Next, we will add the required packages for our server: express, express-graphql, and graphql. Also, we will install the dev dependencies. See Listing 4-2.

Listing 4-2. Packages

```
npm i express express-graphql graphql mongoose cors
npm i -D nodemon dotenv
```

Now, open the folder in VS Code and create a file called .env. Inside it put NODE_ENV and PORT. See Listing 4-3.

Listing 4-3. .env

```
NODE_ENV = 'development'
PORT = 5000
```

Create an Express Server

Now, create an index.js file in the server folder and add the content shown in Listing 4-4 in it. Here, we are first importing the required elements and then listening on a port.

Listing 4-4. index.js

```
const express = require('express');
require('dotenv').config();
const port = process.env.PORT || 5000;

const app = express();
app.listen(port, console.log(`Server running on port
${port}`));
```

Now, we will add the two scripts in the package.json file to start the dev server with the npm run dev command. See Listing 4-5.

Listing 4-5. package.json

```
"scripts": {
  "start": "node server/index.js",
  "dev": "nodemon server/index.js"
},
```

We will also create dummy data for our project by creating a dummyData.js file in the server folder. Here, we have a projects array. It contains different objects with the project details.

In the dummyData.js file, we also have a clients array, which contains data for the clients as objects. See Listing 4-6.

Listing 4-6. dummyData.js

```
// Projects
const projects = [
    {
        id: '1',
        clientId: '1',
        name: 'ReactJS Website',
        description:
            'Lorem ipsum dolor sit amet, consectetuer
            adipiscing elit. Aenean commodo ligula eget
            dolor. Aenean massa. Cum sociis natoque penatibus
            et magnis dis parturient montes, nascetur
            ridiculus mus. Donec quam felis, ultricies nec,
            pellentesque eu.',
        status: 'In Progress',
    },
    ...
];
```

```
// Clients
const clients = [
    {
        id: '1',
        name: 'Fyu Lee',
        email: 'fyulee@gmail.com',
        phone: '343-567-4333',
    },
    ...
];

module.exports = { projects, clients };
```

Set Up GraphQL

Now, we will create a file named schema.js inside a schema folder in the
server folder. Here, we are first importing the dummy data and then the
types required for GraphQL.

In GraphQL, you first have to specify the type for the data. Here, we are
giving the type for the ID, name, email, and phone. Next, we have to create
a RootQuery, which will actually get the data from our dummy file.

In Listing 4-7, we are getting the data of a single client from the
passed-in ID.

Listing 4-7. schema.js

```
const { projects, clients } = require('../dummyData.js');
const { GraphQLObjectType, GraphQLID, GraphQLString,
GraphQLSchema } = require('graphql');

// Client Type
const ClientType = new GraphQLObjectType({
    name: 'Client',
```

```
    fields: () => ({
        id: { type: GraphQLID },
        name: { type: GraphQLString },
        email: { type: GraphQLString },
        phone: { type: GraphQLString },
    }),
});

const RootQuery = new GraphQLObjectType({
    name: 'RootQueryType',
    fields: {
        client: {
            type: ClientType,
            args: { id: { type: GraphQLID } },
            resolve(parent, args) { return clients.find(client
            => client.id === args.id); },
        },
    },
});

module.exports = new GraphQLSchema({ query: RootQuery });
```

Now, in the index.js file, we will import express-graphql and also the schema created earlier. After that, we have to use app.use to specify the endpoint, which is /graphql. See Listing 4-8.

Listing 4-8. index.js

```
const express = require('express');
require('dotenv').config();
const { graphqlHTTP } = require('express-graphql');
const schema = require('./schema/schema');
const port = process.env.PORT || 5000;
```

```
const app = express();

app.use(
    '/graphql',
    graphqlHTTP({
        schema,
        graphiql: process.env.NODE_ENV === 'development',
    })
);

app.listen(port, console.log(`Server running on port
${port}`));
```

Now, start the GraphQL server by running npm run dev from the terminal.

Client Queries

First go to http://localhost:5000/graphql to open GraphQL. See Figure 4-1.

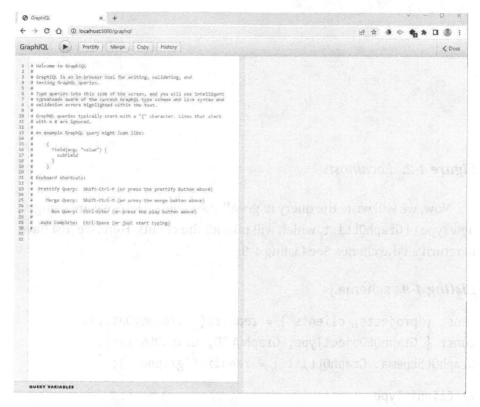

Figure 4-1. *Localhost*

Now, remove everything and give the command shown in Figure 4-2 to get the data for the client with an ID of 1. Notice that we can get all the data or some of the data here.

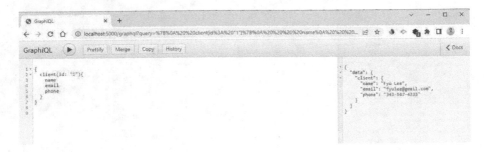

Figure 4-2. *Localhost*

Now, we will write the query to get all the clients. Here, we are using a new type of GraphQLList, which will take all the clients. Here, we just have to return all the clients. See Listing 4-9.

Listing 4-9. schema.js

```
const { projects, clients } = require('../dummyData.js');
const { GraphQLObjectType, GraphQLID, GraphQLString,
GraphQLSchema, GraphQLList } = require('graphql');

// Client Type
const ClientType = new GraphQLObjectType({
  ...
});

const RootQuery = new GraphQLObjectType({
    name: 'RootQueryType',
    fields: {
        clients: {
            type: new GraphQLList(ClientType),
            resolve(parent, args) {
                return clients;
            },
        },
```

```
      client: {
         ...
      },
   },
});

module.exports = new GraphQLSchema({ query: RootQuery });
```

Back in the GraphQL playground, we can simply get all the clients with the following query. Again, we can get any number of fields. See Figure 4-3.

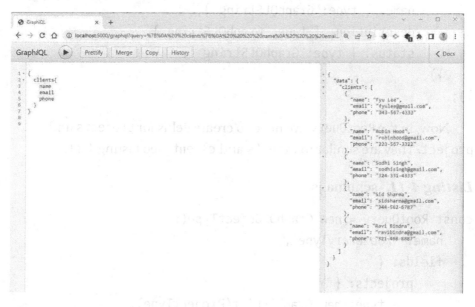

Figure 4-3. *Localhost*

Project Queries

Now, we will create queries for the projects. Here, we need to give a new type called `ProjectType`. Again, we are giving types for the ID, name, description, and status. See Listing 4-10.

Listing 4-10. schema.js

```
const { GraphQLObjectType, GraphQLID, GraphQLString,
GraphQLSchema, GraphQLList } = require('graphql');

// Project Type
const ProjectType = new GraphQLObjectType({
    name: 'Project',
    fields: () => ({
        id: { type: GraphQLID },
        name: { type: GraphQLString },
        description: { type: GraphQLString },
        status: { type: GraphQLString },
    }),
});
```

Now, in the RootQuery, we need to create fields for projects and
project. They are similar to clients and client. See Listing 4-11.

Listing 4-11. schema.js

```
const RootQuery = new GraphQLObjectType({
    name: 'RootQueryType',
    fields: {
        projects: {
            type: new GraphQLList(ProjectType),
            resolve(parent, args) {
                return projects;
            },
        },
        project: {
            type: ProjectType,
            args: { id: { type: GraphQLID } },
```

```
        resolve(parent, args) {
            return projects.find(project => project.id ===
            args.id);
        },
    },
  },
});
```

Now, in the GraphQL playground, we can get the details of all the projects with the project query. See Figure 4-4.

Figure 4-4. *Localhost*

We can also get the details of a single project by passing the ID for a single project. See Figure 4-5.

Figure 4-5. *Localhost*

Each project is associated with a client. So, we will add it as a field in ProjectType. Here, we are finding the client with the clientId value, which is in each project. See Listing 4-12.

Listing 4-12. schema.js

```
const ProjectType = new GraphQLObjectType({
    name: 'Project',
    fields: () => ({
        id: { type: GraphQLID },
        name: { type: GraphQLString },
        description: { type: GraphQLString },
        status: { type: GraphQLString },
        client: {
            type: ClientType,
            resolve(parent, args) {
                return clients.find(client => client.id ===
                parent.clientId);
            },
        },
    }),
});
```

Now, we can get the client associated with each project also from the GraphQL playground. See Figure 4-6.

Figure 4-6. *Localhost*

Cloud MongoDB

Now, we will create a MongoDB database on the cloud. For this, first go to https://account.mongodb.com/account/login and sign up with your Gmail or GitHub account. See Figure 4-7.

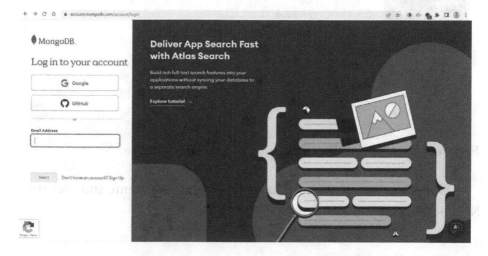

Figure 4-7. *MongoDB*

If you have a lot of databases, then the login will take you to the last database on which you have worked. Click the drop-down and then click the + New Project button. See Figure 4-8.

Figure 4-8. *MongoDB*

On the next screen, we need to give the database a name and click the Next button. See Figure 4-9.

Figure 4-9. *MongoDB*

Now, on the next screen, we will give our email and ask for permission. Here, just click the Create Project button. See Figure 4-10.

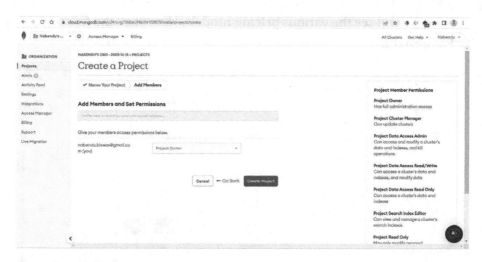

Figure 4-10. *MongoDB*

On the next screen, click the Build a Database button. See Figure 4-11.

Figure 4-11. *MongoDB*

Now, we will see the various pricing models. Here click the free tier. See Figure 4-12.

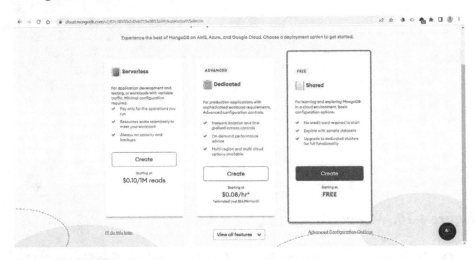

Figure 4-12. *MongoDB*

Now, on the next screen, we can choose the cloud provider and the region of the server. Try to pick a region close to your location. After that, click the Create Cluster button. See Figure 4-13.

Figure 4-13. *MongoDB*

Next, we will be asked for our username and password. Give both of them and click the Create User button. See Figure 4-14.

Figure 4-14. *MongoDB*

Scroll a bit down and click the Add My Current IP Address button. See Figure 4-15.

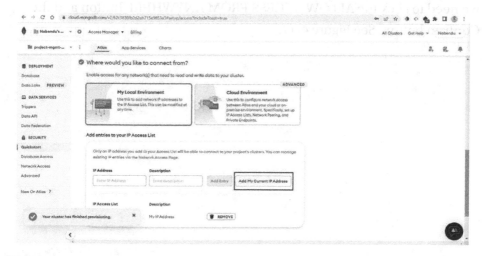

Figure 4-15. *MongoDB*

Now, a pop-up will be shown; click the Go to Databases button. See Figure 4-16.

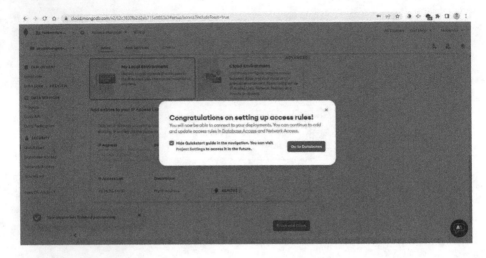

Figure 4-16. *MongoDB*

We need to do one more thing, which is to go to the Network Access tab. Then click the +ADD IP ADDRESS button. It will open a pop-up where we need to click the ALLOW ACCESS FROM ANYWHERE button and the Confirm button. See Figure 4-17.

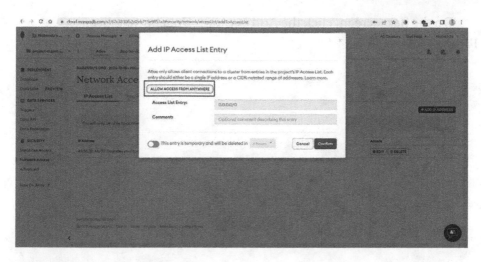

Figure 4-17. *MongoDB*

The database will be created. Click the Browse Collections button. See Figure 4-18.

Figure 4-18. *MongoDB*

On the next screen, click the Add My Own Data button. See Figure 4-19.

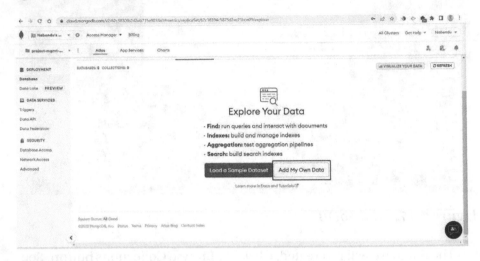

Figure 4-19. *MongoDB*

Now, in the pop-up, give the database a name and also a collection name. After that, click the Create button. See Figure 4-20.

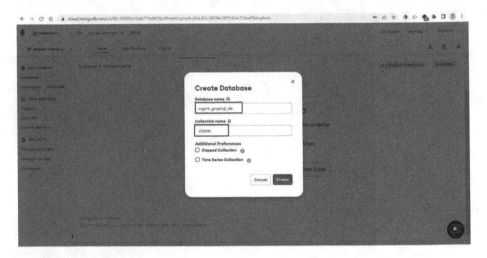

Figure 4-20. *MongoDB*

On the next screen, we will see the database name and the `clients` collection. See Figure 4-21.

Figure 4-21. *MongoDB*

Back on the Database tab, click the Connect button. This will open a pop-up where we click the "Connect your application" link. See Figure 4-22.

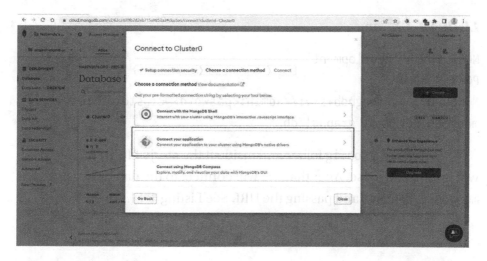

Figure 4-22. *MongoDB*

On the next screen, you will get the link required to get to this database. See Figure 4-23.

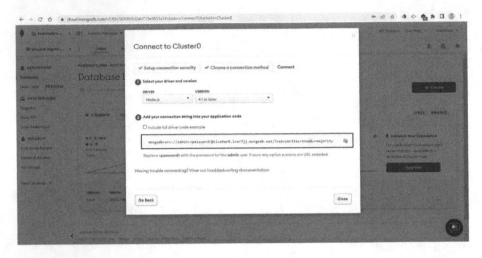

Figure 4-23. *MongoDB*

Now, in the `.env` file, add the `MONGO_URI` variable and the link from earlier. Also provide the correct password here. See Listing 4-13.

Listing 4-13. .env

```
NODE_ENV = 'development'
PORT = 8000
MONGO_URI = 'mongodb+srv://admin:<pasword>@cluster0.bic1vvf.
mongodb.net/mgmt_graphql_db'
```

Next, create a `config` folder and inside it the `db.js` file. Here, we will import `mongoose`. After that, we will connect to the database using `mongoose.connect` and passing the URI. See Listing 4-14.

Listing 4-14. db.js

```
const mongoose = require('mongoose');

const connectDB = async () => {
    const conn = await mongoose.connect(process.env.MONGO_URI);
    console.log(`MongoDB Connected: ${conn.connection.host}`);
};

module.exports = connectDB;
```

Back in the index.js file, we will import the function from the db.js file. After that, we will call it. See Listing 4-15.

Listing 4-15. index.js

```
const schema = require('./schema/schema');
const dbConnect = require('./config/db');
const port = process.env.PORT || 5000;

const app = express();

dbConnect();

app.use(
);

app.listen(port, console.log(`Server running on port
${port}`));
```

Finally, run the command npm run dev, and the successful console log will be displayed. See Figure 4-24.

Figure 4-24. *MongoDB*

Mongoose Models and Fetching Data

Now, create a models folder and two files called Client.js and Project.js
inside it. In the Client.js file, put the schema for the MongoDB database.
These data types are for MongoDB. See Listing 4-16.

Listing 4-16. Client.js

```
const mongoose = require('mongoose');

const ClientSchema = new mongoose.Schema({
    name: {
        type: String,
    },
    email: {
        type: String,
    },
    phone: {
        type: String,
    },
});

module.exports = mongoose.model('Client', ClientSchema);
```

Next, we will add the types in the `Project.js` file. Here, notice that we have an enum type for the status and also a reference to the client. See Listing 4-17.

Listing 4-17. Project.js

```
const mongoose = require('mongoose');

const ProjectSchema = new mongoose.Schema({
    name: {
        type: String,
    },
    description: {
        type: String,
    },
    status: {
        type: String,
        enum: ['Not Started', 'In Progress', 'Completed'],
    },
    clientId: {
        type: mongoose.Schema.Types.ObjectId,
        ref: 'Client',
    },
});

module.exports = mongoose.model('Project', ProjectSchema);
```

Now, we will use these models to fetch data from MongoDB. Here, we will first import the `Client` and `Project` models. Then in the `ProjectType`, we will use the MongoDB command of `findById()` to get the `clientId`. See Listing 4-18.

Listing 4-18. schema.js

```
const Project = require('../models/Project');
const Client = require('../models/Client');
const { GraphQLObjectType, GraphQLID, GraphQLString,
GraphQLSchema, GraphQLList } = require('graphql');

// Project Type
const ProjectType = new GraphQLObjectType({
    name: 'Project',
    fields: () => ({
        id: { type: GraphQLID },
        name: { type: GraphQLString },
        description: { type: GraphQLString },
        status: { type: GraphQLString },
        client: {
            type: ClientType,
            resolve(parent, args) {
                return Client.findById(parent.clientId);
            },
        },
    }),
});
```

Next, we will also update the RootQuery with all the MongoDB commands in the schema.js file. See Listing 4-19.

Listing 4-19. schema.js

```
const RootQuery = new GraphQLObjectType({
    name: 'RootQueryType',
    fields: {
        projects: {
            type: new GraphQLList(ProjectType),
```

```
        resolve(parent, args) {
            return Project.find();
        },
    },
    project: {
        type: ProjectType,
        args: { id: { type: GraphQLID } },
        resolve(parent, args) {
            return Project.findById(args.id);
        },
    },
    clients: {
        type: new GraphQLList(ClientType),
        resolve(parent, args) {
            return Client.find();
        },
    },
    client: {
        type: ClientType,
        args: { id: { type: GraphQLID } },
        resolve(parent, args) {
            return Project.Client(args.id);
        },
    },
    },
  },
});
```

We forgot to add the .env file in .gitignore. So, we will do it next by creating an .env variable in the root directory and adding the content from Listing 4-20 in it.

Listing 4-20. .gitignore

```
node_modules
.env
```

Client Mutations

We will start creating the mutations now, which will be responsible for inserting data in the database. First in the schema.js file, add the import for GraphQLNonNull.

Now, we will create a new mutation type. Here, we will create the addClient mutation by giving it the types first. After that, we will create its resolver to add the name, email, and phone data to the client. See Listing 4-21.

Listing 4-21. schema.js

```
const Project = require('../models/Project');
const Client = require('../models/Client');
const { GraphQLObjectType, GraphQLID, GraphQLString,
GraphQLSchema, GraphQLList, GraphQLNonNull } =
require('graphql');

// Mutations
const mutation = new GraphQLObjectType({
    name: 'Mutation',
    fields: {
        addClient: {
            type: ClientType,
            args: {
                name: { type: GraphQLNonNull(GraphQLString) },
                email: { type: GraphQLNonNull(GraphQLString) },
                phone: { type: GraphQLNonNull(GraphQLString) },
            },
```

```
        resolve(parent, args) {
            const client = new Client({
                name: args.name,
                email: args.email,
                phone: args.phone,
            });
            return client.save();
        },
    }
  }
})

module.exports = new GraphQLSchema({ query: RootQuery,
mutation });
```

Now, in the GraphQL playground, we can use the addClient mutation by passing the name, email, and phone fields. We are also getting back some of the fields. See Figure 4-25.

Figure 4-25. *GraphQL*

We can also check in MongoDB, and the record will be inserted. See Figure 4-26.

Figure 4-26. *MongoDB*

Now, we will add a `deleteClient` mutation, which will use the `findByIdAndRemove` method from MongoDB to remove a field with the ID that was passed. See Listing 4-22.

Listing 4-22. schema.js

```
// Mutations
const mutation = new GraphQLObjectType({
    name: 'Mutation',
    fields: {
        addClient: {
        ...
        },
        deleteClient: {
            type: ClientType,
            args: {
                id: { type: GraphQLNonNull(GraphQLID) },
            },
```

```
        resolve(parent, args) {
            return Client.findByIdAndRemove(args.id);
        },
    }
  }
})
```

Next, we will use it to delete one of the records in the GraphQL playground. See Figure 4-27.

Figure 4-27. *GraphQL*

Project Mutations

We will now write mutations for projects in the schema.js file. Now, we will write an addProject mutation, which is similar to the addClient mutation. Here, we are saving the name, description, status, and clientId fields in the project. Also, notice that for the status, we are taking an enum type.

We also have to import GraphQLEnumType in our imports in the schema.js file. See Listing 4-23.

Listing 4-23. schema.js

```
const { GraphQLObjectType, GraphQLID, GraphQLString,
GraphQLSchema, GraphQLList, GraphQLNonNull, GraphQLEnumType } =
require('graphql');
```

```
// Mutations
const mutation = new GraphQLObjectType({
    name: 'Mutation',
    fields: {
        addClient: {
            ...
        },
        deleteClient: {
          ...
        }
        addProject: {
            type: ProjectType,
            args: {
                name: { type: GraphQLNonNull(GraphQLString) },
                description: { type: GraphQLNonNull
                (GraphQLString) },
                status: {
                    type: new GraphQLEnumType({
                        name: 'ProjectStatus',
                        values: {
                            new: { value: 'Not Started' },
                            progress: { value: 'In Progress' },
                            completed: { value: 'Completed' },
                        },
                    }), defaultValue: 'Not Started',
                },
                clientId: { type: GraphQLNonNull(GraphQLID) },
            },
            resolve(parent, args) {
```

```
                        const project = new Project({ name: args.name,
                        description: args.description,status: args.
                        status, clientId: args.clientId
                        });
                        return project.save();
                    },
                },
            }
        })
```

Now, in the GraphQL playground, we can run the mutation to
addProject by passing the name, description, status, and clientId
fields. See Figure 4-28.

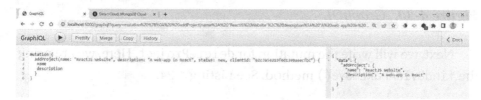

Figure 4-28. *GraphQL*

Now, we can see the project has been added using the projects query.
See Figure 4-29.

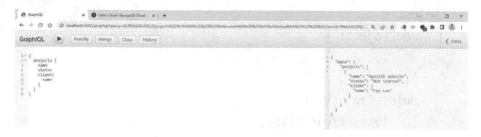

Figure 4-29. *GraphQL*

We have added three more projects with the `addProject` mutation. Now, we can see all of them by using the `projects` query. See Figure 4-30.

Figure 4-30. *GraphQL*

Next, we will write the mutation for `deleteProject`. Here, we are using the `findByIdAndRemove()` method. See Listing 4-24.

Listing 4-24. schema.js

```
// Mutations
const mutation = new GraphQLObjectType({
    name: 'Mutation',
    fields: {
        addProject: {
            ...
        },
        deleteProject: {
            type: ProjectType,
            args: {
                id: { type: GraphQLNonNull(GraphQLID) },
            },
```

```
        resolve(parent, args) {
            return Project.findByIdAndRemove(args.id);
        },
    },
  }
})
```

Now, we can delete a project with the `deleteProject` mutation, by passing the ID. See Figure 4-31.

Figure 4-31. *GraphQL*

We can check and the delete a project with the `projects` query to get rid of it. See Figure 4-32.

Figure 4-32. *GraphQL*

Now, we will write the mutation for updateProject. Here, we need to pass the ID and also the name, description, and status fields. See Listing 4-25.

Listing 4-25. schema.js

```
// Mutations
const mutation = new GraphQLObjectType({
    name: 'Mutation',
    fields: {
        deleteProject: {
            ...
        },
        updateProject: {
            type: ProjectType,
            args: {
                id: { type: GraphQLNonNull(GraphQLID) },
                name: { type: GraphQLString },
                description: { type: GraphQLString },
                status: {
                    type: new GraphQLEnumType({
                        name: 'ProjectStatusUpdate',
                        values: {
                            new: { value: 'Not Started' },
                            progress: { value: 'In Progress' },
                            completed: { value: 'Completed' },
                        },
                    }),
                },
            },
```

```
        resolve(parent, args) {
            return Project.findByIdAndUpdate(
                args.id,
                {
                    $set: {
                        name: args.name,
                        description: args.description,
                        status: args.status,
                    },
                },
                { new: true }
            );
        },
    },
}
})
```

Back in the GraphQL playground, we are using updateProject and passing id and status. On success, we are getting back the name and status. See Figure 4-33.

Figure 4-33. GraphQL

Before moving to the front end, we will also add cors in our index.js file. See Listing 4-26.

Listing 4-26. schema.js

```
const express = require('express');
const cors = require('cors');

...

dbConnect();
app.use(cors());

app.use(
  ...
);

app.listen(port, console.log(`Server running on port
${port}`));
```

Client with React

We will start with our client by giving the npx command to create a React app. Here, we are creating a React app with the name client inside the graphql-project-mgmt folder. See Listing 4-27.

Listing 4-27. Terminal

```
npx create-react-app client
```

After the React app is created, we will change to the directory and add the packages for the Apollo client: graphql, react-router-dom, and react-icons. See Listing 4-28.

Listing 4-28. Terminal

```
npm i @apollo/client graphql react-router-dom react-icons
```

We will do some cleanup by removing the unnecessary files created by React. See Figure 4-34.

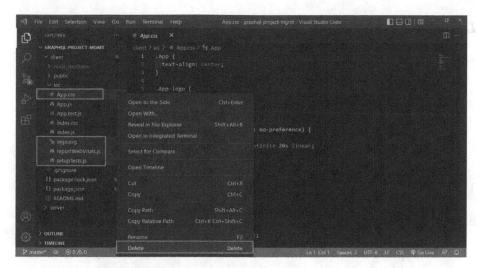

Figure 4-34. *Deleting files*

Now, in the index.js file, we will delete the unnecessary imports, so the file will look like Listing 4-29.

Listing 4-29. index.js

```
import React from 'react';
import ReactDOM from 'react-dom/client';
import './index.css';
import App from './App';

const root = ReactDOM.createRoot(document.
getElementById('root'));
root.render(
  <>
    <App />
  </>·
);
```

Also in the App.js file we will remove everything and just keep a simple h1. See Listing 4-30.

Listing 4-30. App.js

```
function App() {
  return (
    <div className="container">
      <h1>Hello GraphQL</h1>
    </div>
  );
}

export default App;
```

Next, replace the content of the index.css file with Listing 4-31. We have also added a logo.png file in an assets folder inside the components folder.

Listing 4-31. index.css

```
@import url('https://fonts.googleapis.com/css2?family=Finlandic
a:wght@400;600;700&display=swap');

body {
  margin: 0;
  font-family: 'Finlandica', Arial, Helvetica, sans-serif;
}

code {
  font-family: 'Courier New', monospace;
}

.navbar-brand {
  color: #0815a6;
}
```

```css
.navbar-brand img {
  width: 30px;
  margin-right: 10px;
}

.btn {
  font-size: 15px;
}

.btn-primary,
.bg-primary {
  background-color: #0815a6 !important;
  border: none;
}

.btn-primary:hover {
  background-color: #0815a6;
  opacity: 0.9;
}

.btn-secondary {
  background-color: darkmagenta;
}

.btn-secondary:hover {
  background-color: darkmagenta;
  opacity: 0.9;
}

.icon {
  margin-right: 5px;
}
```

We will also add the link and script tags for bootstrapping in the index.html file. See Listing 4-32.

Listing 4-32. index.html

```
<!DOCTYPE html>
<html lang="en">
  <head>
    ...
    <link rel="manifest" href="%PUBLIC_URL%/manifest.json" />
    <link href="https://cdn.jsdelivr.net/npm/bootstrap@5.2.0-
    beta1/dist/css/bootstrap.min.css" rel="stylesheet"
      integrity="sha384-0evHe/X+R7YkIZDRvuzKMRqM+OrBnVFBL6DOitf
      Pri4tjfHxaWutUpFmBp4vmVor" crossorigin="anonymous" />
    <script src="https://cdn.jsdelivr.net/npm/bootstrap@5.2.0-
    beta1/dist/js/bootstrap.bundle.min.js"
      integrity="sha384-pprn3073KE6tl6bjs2QrFaJGz5/
      SUsLqktiwsUTF55Jfv3qYSDhgCecCxMW52nD2"
      crossorigin="anonymous"></script>
    <title>Project Management</title>
  </head>
  <body>
    <noscript>You need to enable JavaScript to run this app.
    </noscript>
    <div id="root"></div>
  </body>
</html>
```

Now, create a `Header.js` file inside the `components` folder. Here, we are using some simple bootstrap classes. See Listing 4-33.

Listing 4-33. Header.js

```
import React from 'react'
import logo from './assets/logo.png';

const Header = () => {
    return (
        <nav className='navbar bg-light mb-4 p-0'>
            <div className='container'>
                <a className='navbar-brand' href='/'>
                    <div className='d-flex'>
                        <img src={logo} alt='logo'
                        className='mr-2' />
                        <div>Project Management</div>
                    </div>
                </a>
            </div>
        </nav>
    );
}

export default Header
```

We will also include the Header component in our App.js file. See
Listing 4-34.

Listing 4-34. App.js

```
import Header from "./components/Header";

function App() {
  return (
    <>
```

```
    <Header />
    <div className="container">
      <h1>Hello GraphQL</h1>
    </div>
  </>
);
}
```

```
export default App;
```

Start the React project by giving npm start in the client folder. Now go to http://localhost:3000 to see our beautiful header. See Figure 4-35.

Hello GraphQL

Figure 4-35. Localhost

Apollo Setup for the Client

To set up Apollo for the client, we need to go to App.js. Here, we will first import ApolloProvider, ApolloClient, and InMemoryCache from the Apollo client.

Next, we will create an instance of ApolloClient and pass our Apollo Server URI and cache.

After that, we will wrap our whole application with ApolloProvider and also pass the client to it. See Listing 4-35.

Listing 4-35. App.js

```
import { ApolloProvider, ApolloClient, InMemoryCache } from
'@apollo/client';
import Header from "./components/Header";
```

```
const client = new ApolloClient({
  uri: 'http://localhost:5000/graphql',
  cache: new InMemoryCache(),
});

function App() {
  return (
    <>
      <ApolloProvider client={client}>
        <Header />
        <div className="container">
          <h1>Hello GraphQL</h1>
        </div>
      </ApolloProvider>
    </>
  );
}

export default App;
```

Now, create a file called `Clients.js` in the components folder and add the required imports in it.

After that, we will add the content for the components. Here, we are getting the data in the `clients` array and mapping through the array. After that, we are passing the single item of array to the `ClientRow` component. See Listing 4-36.

Listing 4-36. Clients.js

```
import { useQuery } from '@apollo/client';
import ClientRow from './ClientRow';
import Spinner from './Spinner';
import { GET_CLIENTS } from './queries';
```

```
const Clients = () => {
    const { loading, error, data } = useQuery(GET_CLIENTS);
    if (loading) return <Spinner />;
    if (error) return <p>Something Went Wrong</p>;
    return (
        <>{!loading && !error && (
                <table className='table table-hover mt-3'>
                    <thead>
                        <tr>
                            <th>Name</th>
                            <th>Email</th>
                            <th>Phone</th>
                            <th></th>
                        </tr>
                    </thead>
                    <tbody>
                        {data.clients.map((client) =>
                        <ClientRow key={client.id}
                        client={client} />)}
                    </tbody>
                </table>
            )}
        </>
    );
}
export default Clients
```

Now, we will create a queries.js file in the component folder and add the getClients query to get the data. See Listing 4-37.

Listing 4-37. queries.js

```
import { gql } from '@apollo/client';

const GET_CLIENTS = gql`
    query getClients {
        clients {
            id
            name
            email
            phone
        }
    }
`;

export { GET_CLIENTS };
```

Now, create a ClientRow.js file in the components folder. Here, we are getting the client props and displaying it, along with an icon. See Listing 4-38.

Listing 4-38. ClientRow.js

```
import { FaTrash } from 'react-icons/fa';
import React from 'react'

const ClientRow = ({ client }) => {
    return (
        <tr>
            <td>{client.name}</td>
            <td>{client.email}</td>
            <td>{client.phone}</td>
```

```
            <td>
                <button className='btn btn-danger btn-sm'>
                    <FaTrash />
                </button>
            </td>
        </tr>
    );
}
```

```
export default ClientRow
```

Now, we will create the `Spinner.js` file inside the `components` folder. Here, we are showing a simple spinner using bootstrap. See Listing 4-39.

Listing 4-39. Spinner.js

```
import React from 'react'

const Spinner = () => {
    return (
        <div className='d-flex justify-content-center'>
            <div className='spinner-border' role='status'>
                <span className='sr-only'></span>
            </div>
        </div>
    );
}
```

```
export default Spinner
```

Finally, we will show the `Clients` component in our `App.js` file. See Listing 4-40.

Listing 4-40. App.js

```
import Clients from './components/Clients';
..

function App() {
  return (
    <>
      <ApolloProvider client={client}>
        <Header />
        <div className="container">
          <Clients />
        </div>
      </ApolloProvider>
    </>
  );
}
export default App;
```

We are able to see our two clients in localhost. See Figure 4-36.

Figure 4-36. *Localhost*

Adding the deleteClient and addClient Mutations

Now, we will create the mutations for the client to delete and add client data. First create a mutations.js file in the components folder. Here, we are creating a deleteClient mutation, where we are passing the ID. See Listing 4-41.

Listing 4-41. mutations.js

```
import { gql } from '@apollo/client';

const DELETE_CLIENT = gql`
    mutation deleteClient($id: ID!) {
        deleteClient(id: $id) {
            id
            name
            email
            phone
        }
    }
`;

export { DELETE_CLIENT }
```

In the `ClientRow.js` file, we will use the `useMutation` hook from the Apollo client to call the `DELETE_CLIENT` mutation when we click the Delete button. Also, notice that we are using `refetchQueries` to get all the client data after a delete. If we don't do this, we have to update the client manually. See Listing 4-42.

Listing 4-42. ClientRow.js

```
import { useMutation } from '@apollo/client';
import { DELETE_CLIENT } from './mutations';
import { GET_CLIENTS } from './queries';

const ClientRow = ({ client }) => {
    const [deleteClient] = useMutation(DELETE_CLIENT, {
        variables: { id: client.id },
        refetchQueries: [{ query: GET_CLIENTS }]
    });
```

```
return (
    <tr>
        ...
        <td>
            <button className='btn btn-danger btn-sm'
            onClick={deleteClient}>
                <FaTrash />
            </button>
        </td>
    </tr>
);
}

export default ClientRow
```

So, now go ahead and delete a client from the front end. See Figure 4-37.

Figure 4-37. *Localhost*

Next, create an AddClient.js file in the components folder. Here, we are using useState to set three fields. After that, we have a button inside the return info to add a client.

In the AddClient.js file, we will create a simple bootstrap modal to fill in all the fields. See Listing 4-43.

Listing 4-43. AddClient.js

```
import React, { useState } from 'react'
import { FaUser } from 'react-icons/fa';

const AddClient = () => {
    const [name, setName] = useState('');
    const [email, setEmail] = useState('');
    const [phone, setPhone] = useState('');

    const onSubmit = e => {
        e.preventDefault();
        console.log(name, email, phone);
    }

    return (
        <>
            <button type='button' className='btn btn-
            secondary' data-bs-toggle='modal' data-bs-
            target='#addClientModal'>
                <div className='d-flex align-items-center'>
                    <FaUser className='icon' />
                    <div>Add Client</div>
                </div>
            </button>
            <div className='modal fade' id='addClientModal'
            aria-labelledby='addClientModalLabel' aria-
            hidden='true'>
                <div className='modal-dialog'>
                    <div className='modal-content'>
                        <div className='modal-header'>
                            <h5 className='modal-title'
                            id='addClientModalLabel'>Add
                            Client</h5>
```

```
    <button type='button'
    className='btn-close' data-
    bs-dismiss='modal' aria-
    label='Close'></button>
</div>
<div className='modal-body'>
    <form onSubmit={onSubmit}>
        <div className='mb-3'>
            <label className='form-
            label'>Name</label>
            <input type='text'
            className='form-control'
            id='name' value={name}
                onChange={(e) =>
                setName(e.target.
                value)} />
        </div>
        <div className='mb-3'>
            <label className='form-
            label'>Email</label>
            <input type='email'
            className='form-control'
            id='email' value={email}
                onChange={(e) =>
                setEmail(e.target.
                value)} />
        </div>
        <div className='mb-3'>
            <label className='form-
            label'>Phone</label>
```

```
                            <input type='text'
                            className='form-control'
                            id='phone' value={phone}
                                onChange={(e) =>
                                setPhone(e.target.
                                value)} />
                        </div>
                        <button type='submit' data-bs-
                        dismiss='modal' className='btn
                        btn-secondary'>Submit</button>
                    </form>
                </div>
            </div>
        </div>
    </>
    )
}

export default AddClient
```

Now, we will add the AddClient component in the App.js file. See Listing 4-44.

Listing 4-44. App.js

```
import Clients from './components/Clients';
import AddClient from './components/AddClient';

function App() {
  return (
    <>
      <ApolloProvider client={client}>
        <Header />
        <div className="container">
```

```
        <AddClient />
        <Clients />
      </div>
    </ApolloProvider>
  </>
  );
}

export default App;
```

When we click the Add Client button, we will get the pop-up. See
Figure 4-38.

Figure 4-38. *Localhost*

Now, in the mutations.js file, we will add the addClient mutation.
Here, we are adding the name, email, and phone. See Listing 4-45.

Listing 4-45. mutations.js

```
const ADD_CLIENT = gql`
    mutation addClient($name: String!, $email: String!, $phone:
    String!) {
        addClient(name: $name, email: $email, phone: $phone) {
            id
            name
```

```
            email
            phone
        }
    }
`;
```

```
export { DELETE_CLIENT, ADD_CLIENT }
```

Next, in the `AddClient.js` file, we will again use the `useMutation` hook from the Apollo client to call the `ADD_CLIENT` mutation. Also, notice that we are using `refetchQueries` to get all the client data after an addition.

We are calling `addClient()` when the user clicks the Submit button. Here, we are also setting the name, email, and phone to an empty string. See Listing 4-46.

Listing 4-46. AddClient.js

```
import { FaUser } from 'react-icons/fa';
import { ADD_CLIENT } from './mutations';
import { GET_CLIENTS } from './queries';
import { useMutation } from '@apollo/client';

const AddClient = () => {
    const [name, setName] = useState('');
    const [email, setEmail] = useState('');
    const [phone, setPhone] = useState('');

    const [addClient] = useMutation(ADD_CLIENT, {
        variables: { name, email, phone }, refetchQueries: [{
        query: GET_CLIENTS }]
    });
```

```
const onSubmit = e => {
    e.preventDefault();
    if (name === '' || email === '' || phone === '') return
    alert('Please fill in all fields');
    addClient(name, email, phone);
    setName('');
    setEmail('');
    setPhone('');
}

return ()
```

Now, we can successfully add a client from the front end. See Figure 4-39.

Figure 4-39. *Localhost*

Displaying Projects and the React Router

Next, we create the query to get all the projects in the queries.js file. See Listing 4-47.

Listing 4-47. queries.js

```
const GET_PROJECTS = gql`
    query getProjects {
        projects {
            id
```

```
            name
            status
        }
    }
`;
```

```
export { GET_CLIENTS, GET_PROJECTS };
```

Now, we will create a Projects.js file in the components folder. Here, we are getting the data by using the useQuery hook. After that, we are mapping through it and sending an individual project to the ProjectCard component. See Listing 4-48.

Listing 4-48. Projects.js

```
import { useQuery } from '@apollo/client';
import ProjectCard from './ProjectCard';
import { GET_PROJECTS } from './queries';
import Spinner from './Spinner';

const Projects = () => {
    const { loading, error, data } = useQuery(GET_PROJECTS);
    if (loading) return <Spinner />;
    if (error) return <p>Something Went Wrong</p>;

    return (
        <>
            {data.projects.length > 0 ? (
                <div className='row mt-4'>
                    {data.projects.map((project) => (
                        <ProjectCard key={project.id}
                        project={project} />
                    ))}
                </div>
            ) : (<p>No Projects</p>)}
```

```
            </>
    );
}
```

```
export default Projects
```

Next, we will create a simple `ProjectCard.js` file in the `components` folder. Here, we are using the `name`, `id`, and `status` fields from the props project. See Listing 4-49.

Listing 4-49. ProjectCard.js

```
import React from 'react'

const ProjectCard = ({ project }) => {
    return (
        <div className='col-md-6'>
            <div className='card mb-3'>
                <div className='card-body'>
                    <div className='d-flex justify-content-
                    between align-items-center'>
                        <h5 className='card-title'>{project.
                        name}</h5>

                        <a className='btn btn-light'
                        href={`/projects/${project.id}`}>
                            View
                        </a>
                    </div>
                    <p className='small'>
                        Status: <strong>{project.
                        status}</strong>
                    </p>
                </div>
```

```
                </div>
            </div>
        )
}
```

```
export default ProjectCard
```

Now, we will show the `Projects` component in the `App.js` file. See Listing 4-50.

Listing 4-50. App.js

```
import Projects from './components/Projects';

const client = new ApolloClient({
    ...
});

function App() {
  return (
    <>
      <ApolloProvider client={client}>
        <Header />
        <div className="container">
          <Projects />
          <AddClient />
          <Clients />
        </div>
      </ApolloProvider>
    </>
  );
}
```

```
export default App;
```

Now, we will also see the projects in localhost. See Figure 4-40.

Figure 4-40. *Localhost*

We will now implement the React Router in our project. Here, we will wrap all the components with `Router` in the `App.js` file. We will then define the route inside `Routes`. Here, we also have a wildcard route to show a single project. See Listing 4-51.

Listing 4-51. App.js

```
import { ApolloProvider, ApolloClient, InMemoryCache } from
'@apollo/client';
import Header from "./components/Header";
import Home from './components/Home';
import Project from './components/Project';
import NotFound from './components/NotFound';
import { BrowserRouter as Router, Route, Routes } from
'react-router-dom';

function App() {
  return (
    <>
      <ApolloProvider client={client}>
        <Router>
          <Header />
```

```
        <div className="container">
          <Routes>
            <Route path='/' element={<Home />} />
            <Route path='/projects/:id'
            element={<Project />} />
            <Route path='*' element={<NotFound />} />
          </Routes>
        </div>
      </Router>
    </ApolloProvider>
  </>
);
}

export default App;
```

Now, we will move the components of AddClient, Projects, and Clients inside a Home.js file. See Listing 4-52.

Listing 4-52. Home.js

```
import AddClient from './AddClient'
import AddProject from './AddProject'
import Clients from './Clients'
import Projects from './Projects'

const Home = () => {
    return (
    <>
            <div className='d-flex gap-3 mb-4'>
                <AddProject />
                <AddClient />
            </div>
```

```
        <Projects />
        <hr />
        <Clients />
    </>
    )
}
```

export default Home

We will also create a NotFound.js file inside the components folder. Here, we will just show a static file, containing 404 text. See Listing 4-53.

Listing 4-53. NotFound.js

```
import { FaExclamationTriangle } from 'react-icons/fa';
import { Link } from 'react-router-dom';

const NotFound = () => {
    return (
        <div className='d-flex flex-column justify-content-
        center align-items-center mt-5'>
            <FaExclamationTriangle className='text-danger'
            size='5em' />
            <h1>404</h1>
            <h4 className='lead'>Page does not exist</h4>
            <Link to='/' className='btn btn-success'>Go
            Back</Link>
        </div>
    )
}

export default NotFound
```

Now, when we go to any nonexistent page, we will see the 404 text. See
Figure 4-41.

Figure 4-41. NotFound

Displaying a Single Project

Now, we will create a query to get the details of a single project in the
queries.js file. Here, we need to pass the ID of the project. We are getting
back the project description, along with the client of the project. See
Listing 4-54.

Listing 4-54. queries.js

```
const GET_PROJECT = gql`
    query getProject($id: ID!) {
        project(id: $id) {
        id
        name
        description
        status
        client {
            id
            name
            email
            phone
            }
```

```
        }
    }
`;
```

```
export { GET_CLIENTS, GET_PROJECTS, GET_PROJECT };
```

Now, we will create a new `Project.js` file in the components folder. Here, we are again using the `useQuery` hook to get the details of a project and storing it in the data variable.

Inside the return info, we are just showing the details. See Listing 4-55.

Listing 4-55. Project.js

```
import { useQuery } from '@apollo/client';
import { Link, useParams } from 'react-router-dom';
import { GET_PROJECT } from './queries';
import Spinner from './Spinner';

const Project = () => {
    const { id } = useParams();
    const { loading, error, data } = useQuery(GET_PROJECT, {
    variables: { id } });
    if (loading) return <Spinner />;
    if (error) return <p>Something Went Wrong</p>;

    return (
        <>
            {!loading && !error && (
                <div className='mx-auto w-75 card p-5'>
                    <Link to='/' className='btn btn-dark btn-sm
                    w-15 d-inline ms-auto'>Back</Link>
                    <h1>{data.project.name}</h1>
                    <p>{data.project.description}</p>
                    <h5 className='mt-3'>Project Status</h5>
```

```
                    <p className='lead'>{data.project.
                    status}</p>
                </div>
            )}
        </>
    )
}
```

```
export default Project
```

Now, when we click any project, we will get the details of it. See Figure 4-42.

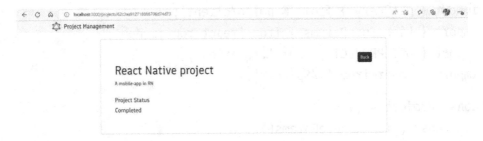

Figure 4-42. *Project*

We will also add the client data in the Project.js file. See Listing 4-56.

Listing 4-56. Project.js

```
import { FaEnvelope, FaPhone, FaIdBadge } from 'react-icons/fa';

const Project = () => {
    const { id } = useParams();
    const { loading, error, data } = useQuery(GET_PROJECT,
    { variables: { id } });
    if (loading) return <Spinner />;
    if (error) return <p>Something Went Wrong</p>;
```

```
    return (
        <>
        {!loading && !error && (
            <div className='mx-auto w-75 card p-5'>
                <Link to='/' className='btn btn-dark btn-sm
                w-15 d-inline ms-auto'>Back</Link>
                <h1>{data.project.name}</h1>
                <p>{data.project.description}</p>
                <h5 className='mt-3'>Project Status</h5>
                <p className='lead'>{data.project.
                status}</p>
                <h5 className='mt-5'>Client
                Information</h5>
                <ul className='list-group'>
                    <li className='list-group-
                    item'><FaIdBadge className='icon' />
                    {data.project.client.name}</li>
                    <li className='list-group-
                    item'><FaEnvelope className='icon' />
                    {data.project.client.email}</li>
                    <li className='list-group-
                    item'><FaPhone className='icon' />
                    {data.project.client.phone}</li>
                </ul>
            </div>
        )}
        </>
    )
}

export default Project
```

Now, we will also get the client information for the project. See Figure 4-43.

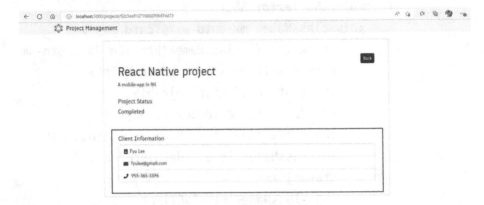

Figure 4-43. *Localhost*

Creating the addProject and deleteProject Mutations

Now, we will create the mutations for projects. First create an AddProject.js file inside the components folder. Here, we are creating the variables for name, description, clientId, and status. We are also getting the client data using the useQuery hook.

Next, inside the return statement, we will create a button called New Project. We will also write the code to display a modal when the button is clicked.

We will complete the form to take the user data. Here, we are also showing a drop-down, which will map through the client data to show the clients. See Listing 4-57.

Listing 4-57. AddProject.js

```
import { useMutation, useQuery } from '@apollo/client';
import React, { useState } from 'react'
import { GET_CLIENTS } from './queries';

const AddProject = () => {
  const [name, setName] = useState('');
  const [description, setDescription] = useState('');
  const [clientId, setClientId] = useState('');
  const [status, setStatus] = useState('new');
  const { loading, error, data } = useQuery(GET_CLIENTS);

  const onSubmit = (e) => {
    e.preventDefault();
    if (name === '' || description === '' || status === '')
    return alert('Please fill in all fields');
    addProject(name, description, clientId, status);
    setName('');
    setDescription('');
    setStatus('new');
    setClientId('');
  };
  if (loading) return null;
  if (error) return 'Something Went Wrong';

  return (
    <>
      {!loading && !error && (
        <>
          <button type='button' className='btn btn-
          primary' data-bs-toggle='modal' data-bs-
          target='#addProjectModal'>
            <div className='d-flex align-items-center'>
```

145

```
    <FaList className='icon' />
    <div>New Project</div>
  </div>
</button>
<div className='modal fade' id='addProjectModal'
aria-labelledby='addProjectModalLabel' aria-
hidden='true'>
  <div className='modal-dialog'>
    <div className='modal-content'>
      <div className='modal-header'>
        <h5 className='modal-title'
        id='addProjectModalLabel'>New Project</h5>
        <button type='button' className='btn-
        close' data-bs-dismiss='modal' aria-
        label='Close'></button>
      </div>
      <div className='modal-body'>
        <form onSubmit={onSubmit}>
          <div className='mb-3'>
            <label className='form-
            label'>Name</label>
            <input type='text' className='form-
            control' id='name' value={name}
              onChange={e => setName(e.target.
              value)} />
          </div>
          <div className='mb-3'>
            <label className='form-
            label'>Description</label>
            <textarea className='form-control'
            id='description' value={description}
```

```
      onChange={e => setDescription(e.target.
      value)}></textarea>
  </div>
  <div className='mb-3'>
    <label className='form-
    label'>Status</label>
    <select id='status' className='form-
    select' value={status}
      onChange={e => setStatus(e.target.
      value)}>
      <option value='new'>Not
      Started</option>
      <option value='progress'>In
      Progress</option>
      <option value='completed'>
      Completed</option>
    </select>
  </div>
  <div className='mb-3'>
    <label className='form-
    label'>Client</label>
    <select id='clientId' className='form-
    select' value={clientId}
      onChange={e => setClientId(e.target.
      value)}>
      <option value=''>Select Client</option>
      {data.clients.map((client) =>
        <option key={client.id}
        value={client.id}>{client.name}
        </option>)}
    </select>
  </div>
```

```
                    <button type='submit' data-bs-
                    dismiss='modal' className='btn btn-
                    primary'>Submit</button>
                  </form>
                </div>
              </div>
            </div>
          </div>
        </>
      )}
    </>
  )
}
```

```
export default AddProject
```

Now, we will add the ADD_PROJECT mutation to add the project in the mutations.js file. See Listing 4-58.

Listing 4-58. mutations.js

```
const ADD_PROJECT = gql`
    mutation addProject($name: String!, $description: String!,
    $status: ProjectStatus!, $clientId: ID!) {
        addProject(name: $name, description: $description,
        status: $status, clientId: $clientId) {
            id
            name
            description
            status
            client {
                id
                name
```

```
            email
            phone
        }
      }
    }
`;

export { DELETE_CLIENT, ADD_CLIENT, ADD_PROJECT }
```

Finally in the AddProject.js file, we will use the addProject mutation. See Listing 4-59.

Listing 4-59. AddProject.js

```
import React, { useState } from 'react'
import { GET_CLIENTS, GET_PROJECTS } from './queries';
import { FaList } from 'react-icons/fa';
import { ADD_PROJECT } from './mutations';

const AddProject = () => {
  const [name, setName] = useState('');
  const [description, setDescription] = useState('');
  const [clientId, setClientId] = useState('');
  const [status, setStatus] = useState('new');
  const { loading, error, data } = useQuery(GET_CLIENTS);

  const [addProject] = useMutation(ADD_PROJECT, {
    variables: { name, description, clientId, status },
    refetchQueries: [{ query: GET_PROJECTS }]
  });
```

Now, in localhost, we will see the new button called New Project. Clicking it will open a pop-up in which we can give the project details. See Figure 4-44.

Figure 4-44. *Localhost*

Now, we can see that the new project was added after we clicked the Submit button in the previous pop-up. See Figure 4-45.

Figure 4-45. *Project*

In the Project.js file, we will call a new component called DeleteProject. See Listing 4-60.

Listing 4-60. Project.js

```
import { FaEnvelope, FaPhone, FaIdBadge } from 'react-icons/fa';
import DeleteProject from './DeleteProject';

const Project = () => {

    return (
        <>
            {!loading && !error && (
                <div className='mx-auto w-75 card p-5'>
                    <ul className='list-group'>
                    </ul>
                    <DeleteProject projectId={data.project.id} />
                </div>
            )}
        </>
    )
}

export default Project
```

Now, we will create the mutation for DELETE_PROJECT inside our mutations.js file. See Listing 4-61.

Listing 4-61. mutations.js

```
const DELETE_PROJECT = gql`
    mutation DeleteProject($id: ID!) {
        deleteProject(id: $id) {
            id
        }
    }
`;

export { DELETE_CLIENT, ADD_CLIENT, ADD_PROJECT, DELETE_PROJECT }
```

Next, we will create a file called DeleteProject.js inside the components folder. Here, we are using the mutation called DELETE_PROJECT when the user clicks the trash icon. See Listing 4-62.

Listing 4-62. DeleteProject.js

```
import { useMutation } from '@apollo/client';
import { FaTrash } from 'react-icons/fa';
import { useNavigate } from 'react-router-dom';
import { DELETE_PROJECT } from './mutations';
import { GET_PROJECTS } from './queries';

const DeleteProject = ({ projectId }) => {
    const navigate = useNavigate();
    const [deleteProject] = useMutation(DELETE_PROJECT, {
        variables: { id: projectId },
        onCompleted: () => navigate('/'),
        refetchQueries: [{ query: GET_PROJECTS }],
    });

    return (
        <div className='d-flex mt-5 ms-auto'>
            <button className='btn btn-danger m-2'
            onClick={deleteProject}>
                <FaTrash className='icon' /> Delete Project
            </button>
        </div>
    );
}

export default DeleteProject
```

Now, click the Delete Project button from inside any project. See Figure 4-46.

Figure 4-46. *Localhost*

We can see that the project has been deleted in the home screen. See Figure 4-47.

Figure 4-47. *Localhost*

Updating the Project and Cascade Delete

Now, we will first add the logic to edit a project. In the Project.js file, we will call a new component called EditProject and pass the project data. See Listing 4-63.

Listing 4-63. Project.js

```
import DeleteProject from './DeleteProject';
import EditProject from './EditProject';

const Project = () => {

    return (
        <>
            {!loading && !error && (
                <div className='mx-auto w-75 card p-5'>
                    <EditProject project={data.project} />
                    <DeleteProject projectId={data.
                    project.id} />
                </div>
            )}
        </>
    )
}

export default Project
```

Next, we will create the UPDATE_PROJECT mutation in the mutations.js file. Here, we are passing the ID, along with other data. See Listing 4-64.

Listing 4-64. mutations.js

```
const UPDATE_PROJECT = gql`
    mutation updateProject($id: ID!, $name: String!,
    $description: String!, $status: ProjectStatusUpdate!) {
```

```
    updateProject(id: $id, name: $name, description:
    $description, status: $status) {
        id
        name
        description
        status
        client {
                id
                name
                email
                phone
        }
    }
}
`;
```

```
export { DELETE_CLIENT, ADD_CLIENT, ADD_PROJECT, DELETE_
PROJECT, UPDATE_PROJECT };
```

Next, we will create a file called `EditProject.js` inside the components folder. Here, we are using the `UPDATE_PROJECT` mutation and passing the ID, name, description, and status.

Now, we will add a form to take the details from the user in the `EditProject.js` file. See Listing 4-65.

Listing 4-65. EditProject.js

```
import { useMutation } from '@apollo/client';
import React, { useState } from 'react'
import { UPDATE_PROJECT } from './mutations';
import { GET_PROJECT } from './queries';
```

```
const EditProject = ({ project }) => {
    const [name, setName] = useState(project.name);
    const [description, setDescription] = useState(project.
    description);
    const [status, setStatus] = useState('');
    const [updateProject] = useMutation(UPDATE_PROJECT, {
        variables: { id: project.id, name, description,
        status },
        refetchQueries: [{ query: GET_PROJECT, variables: { id:
        project.id } }],
    });

    const onSubmit = (e) => {
        e.preventDefault();
        if (!name || !description || !status) {
            return alert('Please fill out all fields');
        }
        updateProject(name, description, status);
    };

    return (
        <div className='mt-5'>
            <h3>Update Project Details</h3>
            <form onSubmit={onSubmit}>
                <div className='mb-3'>
                    <label className='form-label'>Name</label>
                    <input type='text' className='form-control'
                    id='name' value={name} onChange={e =>
                    setName(e.target.value)} />
                </div>
                <div className='mb-3'>
```

```
            <label className='form-
            label'>Description</label>
            <textarea className='form-control'
            id='description' value={description}
            onChange={e => setDescription(e.target.
            value)}></textarea>
        </div>
        <div className='mb-3'>
            <label className='form-label'>Status</label>
            <select id='status' className='form-select'
            value={status} onChange={e => setStatus
            (e.target.value)}>
                <option value='new'>Not
                Started</option>
                <option value='progress'>In
                Progress</option>
                <option value='completed'>Completed
                </option>
            </select>
        </div>
        <button type='submit' className='btn
        btn-primary'>Submit</button>
    </form>
  </div>
 )
}

export default EditProject
```

Inside each project, we will also get the Update Project form. Here, we can update a field and click the Submit button. See Figure 4-48.

Figure 4-48. *Localhost*

Finally, we will add the logic to have cascading deletes. Here, when we delete a client, we will delete all the projects associated with that client. For this we need to update the deleteClient resolver in schema.js of the server. See Listing 4-66.

Listing 4-66. schema.js

```
deleteClient: {
    type: ClientType,
    args: {
        id: { type: GraphQLNonNull(GraphQLID) },
    },
    resolve(parent, args) {
        Project.find({ clientId: args.id
        }).then((projects) => {
            projects.forEach((project) => {
                project.remove();
            });
        });
```

```
        return Client.findByIdAndRemove(args.id);
    },
},
```

Next, in the ClientRow.js file, we will also refetch all the projects. See Listing 4-67.

Listing 4-67. ClientRow.js

```
import { FaTrash } from 'react-icons/fa';
import React from 'react'
import { useMutation } from '@apollo/client';
import { DELETE_CLIENT } from './mutations';
import { GET_CLIENTS, GET_PROJECTS } from './queries';

const ClientRow = ({ client }) => {
    const [deleteClient] = useMutation(DELETE_CLIENT, {
        variables: { id: client.id },
        refetchQueries: [{ query: GET_CLIENTS }, { query:
        GET_PROJECTS }]
    });

    return (
        <tr>
            ...
        </tr>
    );
}

export default ClientRow
```

Now, in localhost, delete a client by clicking the Delete button. See Figure 4-49.

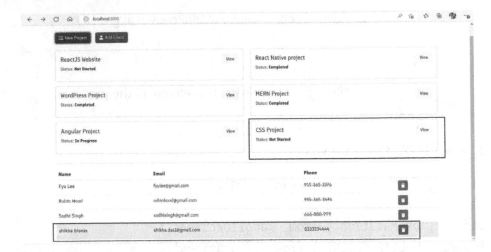

Figure 4-49. *Localhost*

The client and the project associated with the client are deleted. See Figure 4-50.

Figure 4-50. *Localhost*

This completes our project. You can find the code for this at `https://github.com/nabendu82/graphql-project-mgmt`.

Summary

In this chapter, we created a full-stack app with a GraphQL server in the back end, which was connected to the MongoDB database. We also created the front end in ReactJS and connected it to the back end using the Apollo client.

In the next chapter, you will learn about creating an app with Prisma.

CHAPTER 5

Creating an App with Prisma

In this chapter, we will use Prisma to build the back end of a blog app. This is an ORM tool that autogenerates a schema and other things for GraphQL.

The Setup

We will create a new directory called blog-app-prisma. Inside it, we will create another folder named server. In the server folder, we will initialize an empty called package.json by giving the command npm. See Listing 5-1.

Listing 5-1. Terminal

```
mkdir blog-app-prisma
cd blog-app-prisma/
mkdir server
cd server/
npm init -y
```

Next, we will install apollo-server and graphql as the main dependencies and install typescript and ts-node-dev as the dev dependencies. See Listing 5-2.

© Nabendu Biswas 2023

N. Biswas, *Practical GraphQL*, https://doi.org/10.1007/978-1-4842-9621-9_5

Listing 5-2. Packages

```
npm i apollo-server@3.4.0 graphql@15.6.1
npm i -D typescript@4.4.4 ts-node-dev@1.1.8
```

Now, we will create the src folder and an index.js file inside it. We are logging a simple TypeScript variable to the console. See Listing 5-3.

Listing 5-3. index.ts

```
const age: number = 40;
console.log(age);
```

Now, we will run the nodemon command shown in Listing 5-4 to watch for all TypeScript files and execute the index.ts file with ts-node.

Listing 5-4. nodemon

```
nodemon --watch './**/*.ts' --exec 'ts-node' src/index.ts
```

Next, we need to create the TypeScript file configuration in the root directory. Create a file called tsconfig.json and add the content shown in Listing 5-5 in it.

Listing 5-5. tsconfig.json

```
{
    "compilerOptions": {
        "target": "es5",
        "lib": [
            "dom",
            "es6"
        ],
        "module": "commonjs",
        "rootDir": "src",
        "outDir": "dist",
```

```
        "removeComments": true,
        "esModuleInterop": true,
        "forceConsistentCasingInFileNames": true,
        "strict": true,
        "skipLibCheck": true
    }
}
```

Now, in the `index.ts` file, we will write a simple query and resolver. We are also creating a new instance of `ApolloServer` and passing in the query and resolvers. After that, we are listening on the provided URL. See Listing 5-6.

Listing 5-6. index.ts

```
import { ApolloServer, gql } from "apollo-server";

const typeDefs = gql`
    type Query {
        hello: String!
    }
`

const resolvers = {
    Query: {
        hello: () => "Prisma!"
    }
}

const server = new ApolloServer({
    typeDefs, resolvers
})

server.listen().then(({ url }) => {
    console.log(`Server ready on ${url}`);
})
```

165

Now open `http://localhost:4000` in a browser and then click the "Query your server" button. See Figure 5-1.

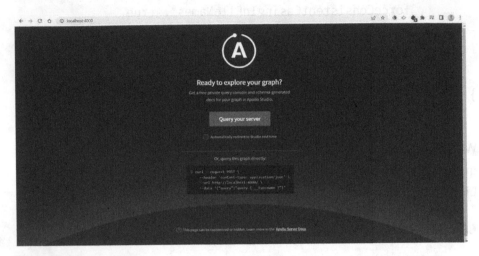

Figure 5-1. *Localhost*

We will go to the sandbox next. Here, we have given a simple query. We run it and get data from it. See Figure 5-2.

Figure 5-2. *Localhost*

We will separate our queries now. First, create a `schema.ts` file in the `src` directory. Here, we have moved `typeDefs` from the `index.ts` file. See Listing 5-7.

Listing 5-7. schema.ts

```
import { gql } from "apollo-server";

export const typeDefs = gql`
    type Query {
        hello: String!
    }
`
```

Now, create a `resolvers` folder inside `src` and create a file named `Query.ts` inside that. Place the query in that file, as shown in Listing 5-8.

Listing 5-8. Query.ts

```
export const Query = {
    hello: () => "Prisma!"
}
```

Back in the `index.ts` file, we will add our `typeDefs` and `Query`. See Listing 5-9.

Listing 5-9. index.ts

```
import { ApolloServer } from "apollo-server";
import { Query } from "./resolvers/Query";
import { typeDefs } from "./schema";

const server = new ApolloServer({
    typeDefs,
    resolvers: {
        Query
    }
})
```

```
server.listen().then(({ url }) => {
    console.log(`Server ready on ${url}`);
})
```

ElephantSQL Setup

We will create an instance of PostgreSQL from ElephantSQL. This is a completely free service that we don't even have to give credit card information to use. They also have a generous free quota. See Figure 5-3.

Figure 5-3. *ElephantSQL*

Now, sign up with your Google or GitHub account and you will see the screen in Figure 5-4. Here, click the Create New Instance button.

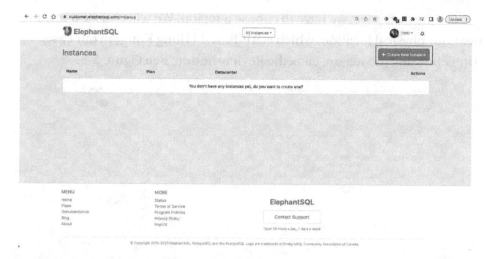

Figure 5-4. *Create New Instance button*

On the next page, we need to give the instance a name, which is `blog-app-prisma` in our case. Also, we give a tag of `prisma`. See Figure 5-5.

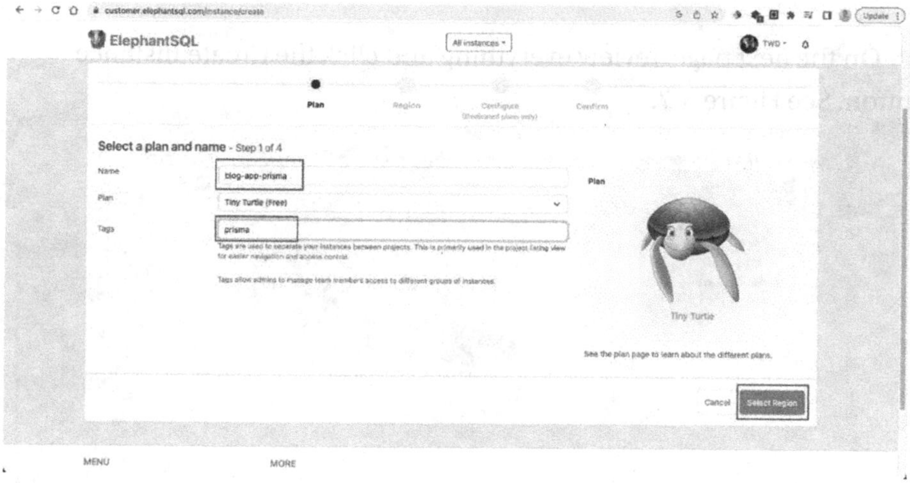

Figure 5-5. *New app*

On the next page, we have to choose a region. We will choose a region near our physical location, which is AP-East-1 (Hong Kong) in our case. After choosing the region, click the Review button. See Figure 5-6.

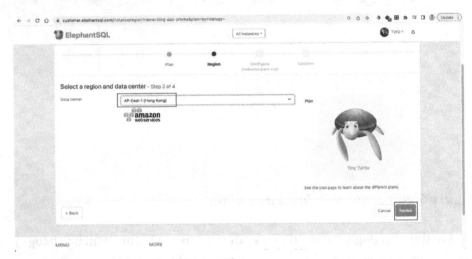

Figure 5-6. *Selecting a region*

On the next page, review everything and click the Create Instance button. See Figure 5-7.

Figure 5-7. *New instance*

Now, our new instance of `blog-app-prisma` is created. We need to click it. See Figure 5-8.

Figure 5-8. *Instance created*

On the next page, copy the URL, which includes the password of this PostgreSQL instance. See Figure 5-9.

Figure 5-9. *Instance details*

Configuring Prisma

We will configure Prisma now by installing it as a dev dependency. See Listing 5-10.

Listing 5-10. Terminal

```
npm i -D prisma@3.3.0
```

Now, from the terminal, give the command `npx prisma init` to set up Prisma. This will create a `schema.prisma` file. See Listing 5-11.

Listing 5-11. Initialize Prisma

```
npx prisma init
```

Now in the `.env` file, add the Postgres URL as `DATABASE_URL`. See Listing 5-12.

Listing 5-12. .env File

```
DATABASE_URL="postgres://aycvagpb:OmjgwmXXXXXX.db.elephantsql.
com/xxxxxxx"
```

We will also create the schema in the `schema.prisma` file. Here, we have a `Post`, `User`, and `Profile`. See Listing 5-13.

Listing 5-13. schema.prisma file

```
model Post {
  id        Int      @id @default(autoincrement())
  title     String
  content   String
  published Boolean  @default(false)
  createdAt DateTime @default(now())
  updatedAt DateTime @updatedAt
}
```

```
model User {
  id        Int        @id @default(autoincrement())
  email     String     @unique
  name      String?
  password  String
  createdAt DateTime @default(now())
  updatedAt DateTime @updatedAt
}

model Profile {
  id        Int        @id @default(autoincrement())
  bio       String
  createdAt DateTime @default(now())
  updatedAt DateTime @updatedAt
}
```

Next, give the command npx prisma db push from the command line to sync the database with the schema. See Listing 5-14.

Listing 5-14. Terminal

```
npx prisma db push
```

Figure 5-10. *Terminal is written*

Prisma comes with Studio so you can see the database. So, we will run npx prisma studio to open it. See Listing 5-15.

173

Listing 5-15. Terminal

```
npx prisma studio
```

This will open the database in `http://localhost:5555`, where we will see all of our models. See Figure 5-11.

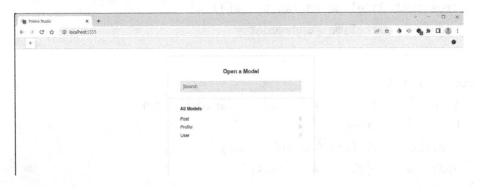

Figure 5-11. *Localhost*

We can check each model by clicking it. See Figure 5-12.

Figure 5-12. *Localhost*

Next, we will update the model for `Post`, `User`, and `Profile` in the `schema.prisma` file. See Listing 5-16.

Listing 5-16. schema.prisma

```
model Post {
  ...
  updatedAt DateTime @updatedAt
  authorId  Int
  author    User     @relation(fields: [authorId],
                       references: [id])
}

model User {
  ...
  updatedAt DateTime @updatedAt
  posts     Post[]
  profile   Profile?
}

model Profile {
  ...
  updatedAt DateTime @updatedAt
  userId    Int      @unique
  user      User     @relation(fields: [userId],
                       references: [id])
}
```

We need to again run the command npx prisma db push from the command line to sync the database with the schema. See Listing 5-17.

Listing 5-17. Terminal

```
npx prisma db push
```

Now, we will see the updated columns in Prisma Studio. See Figure 5-13.

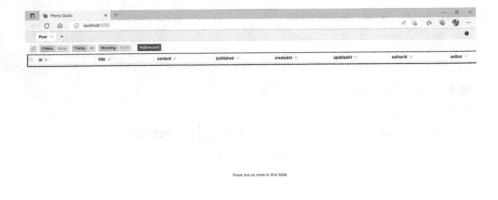

Figure 5-13. *Localhost*

Creating the Schema and First Mutation

We need to create the schema now, which will be required by the GraphQL server. So, create a schema.ts file in the src folder and add the type for Post, User, and Profile in it.

We will also create the type of mutation, UserError and PostPayload, in the schema.ts file. See Listing 5-18.

Listing 5-18. schema.ts

```
import { gql } from "apollo-server";

export const typeDefs = gql`
    type Query {
        hello: String!
    }
```

```
type Mutation{
    postCreate(title: String!, content: String!):
    PostPayload!
}

type UserError {
    message: String!
}

type PostPayload {
    userErrors: [UserError!]!
    post: Post
}

type Post {
    id: ID!
    title: String!
    content: String!
    createdAt: String!
    published: Boolean!
    user: User!
}

type User {
    id: ID!
    name: String!
    email: String!
    profile: Profile!
    posts: [Post!]!
}
```

```
type Profile {
    id: ID!
    bio: String!
    user: User!
}
```

Next, in the index.ts file, we need to import Prisma and the Prisma client and then create an instance of PrismaClient. We are also creating an interface for the context and making it equal to prisma. See Listing 5-19.

Listing 5-19. index.ts

```
import { typeDefs } from "./schema";
import { Prisma, PrismaClient } from "@prisma/client";

const prisma = new PrismaClient();

export interface Context {
    prisma: PrismaClient<
        Prisma.PrismaClientOptions,
        never,
        Prisma.RejectOnNotFound | Prisma.RejectPerOperation |
        undefined
    >
}

const server = new ApolloServer({
    typeDefs,
    resolvers: {
        Query
    },
    context: { prisma }
})
```

Now, we will create our first mutation of postCreate in a file named Mutation.ts.

We will create this file inside a resolvers folder in the src folder.

Here, we are using Prisma to create the post. Since we are using TypeScript, we have to give a type for everything. Here, we are passing the title and content. Also, we are hard-coding the authorId value as of now. See Listing 5-20.

Listing 5-20. Mutation.ts

```
import { Context } from '../index';

interface PostArgs {
    title: string;
    content: string;
}

export const Mutation = {
    postCreate: async (_: any, { title, content }: PostArgs, {
    prisma }: Context) => {
        prisma.post.create({
            data: { title, content, authorId: 1 }
        })
    },
}
```

Next, we will go to the Apollo Sandbox and create some users manually. See Figure 5-14.

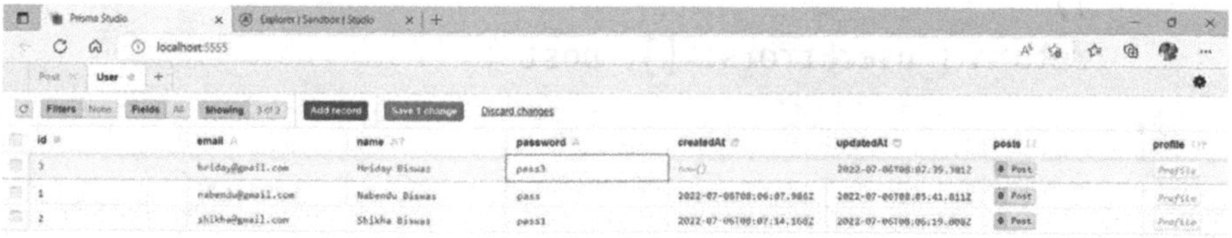

Figure 5-14. *Sandbox*

Now, we will update our mutation of postCreate to include errors also. We will be returning these errors if the user doesn't provide any title or content. See Listing 5-21.

Listing 5-21. Mutation.ts

```
import { Context } from '../index';
import { Post } from '@prisma/client';

interface PostArgs {
    title: string;
    content: string;
}

interface PostPayloadType {
    userErrors: { message: string }[];
    post: Post | null;
}

export const Mutation = {
    postCreate: async (_: any, { title, content }: PostArgs,
    { prisma }: Context): Promise<PostPayloadType> => {
        if(!title || !content) {
            return { userErrors: [{ message: "You must provide
            title and content"}], post: null }
        }
        const post = await prisma.post.create({
            data: { title, content, authorId: 1 }
        })
        return { userErrors: [], post }
    },
}
```

Now, in the index.ts file, we will include the mutation file. See
Listing 5-22.

Listing 5-22. index.ts

```
import { Prisma, PrismaClient } from "@prisma/client";
import { Mutation } from "./resolvers/Mutation";

const prisma = new PrismaClient();

const server = new ApolloServer({
    typeDefs,
    resolvers: {
        Query, Mutation
    },
    context: { prisma }
})
```

Now, we can run our mutation from the GraphQL sandbox and
create it successfully. Note that we need to have the command shown in
Listing 5-23 running and after that go to http://localhost:4000/. See
Figure 5-15.

Listing 5-23. Terminal

```
nodemon --watch './**/*.ts' --exec 'ts-node' src/index.ts
```

Figure 5-15. *GraphQL*

If we don't pass a title, we will get an error. See Figure 5-16.

Figure 5-16. *GraphQL*

Now, we can see that the post has been updated in the database in the Apollo Sandbox. See Figure 5-17.

Figure 5-17. *Sandbox*

More Queries and Mutations

Now, in the schema.ts file, we will update the query to have the type of posts, which is an array of Post. See Listing 5-24.

Listing 5-24. schema.ts

```
import { gql } from "apollo-server";

export const typeDefs = gql`
    type Query {
        posts: [Post!]!
    }
`
```

Now, create a Query.ts file inside the resolvers folder. Here, we are writing a query that is using the prisma method of findMany to get the posts. See Listing 5-25.

Listing 5-25. Query.ts

```
import { Context } from "../index";

export const Query = {
    posts: (_: any, __: any, { prisma }: Context) => {
```

```
        return prisma.post.findMany({
            orderBy: [{ createdAt: "desc" }]
        });
    },
}
```

Now, in the GraphQL sandbox, we can get the posts. See Figure 5-18.

Figure 5-18. *GraphQL*

Now, we will update the postCreate mutation to use an input in the schema.ts file. We have also created another postUpdate mutation. See Listing 5-26.

Listing 5-26. schema.ts

```
export const typeDefs = gql`
    type Query {
        posts: [Post!]!
    }

    type Mutation{
        postCreate(post: PostInput!): PostPayload!
        postUpdate(post: PostInput!): PostPayload!

    }
```

```
type UserError {
    message: String!
}

type PostPayload {
    userErrors: [UserError!]!
    post: Post
}

input PostInput {
    title: String
    content: String
}
```

We will also update our mutation of postCreate to use the new input type. We have also moved prisma.post.create to the return statement. See Listing 5-27.

Listing 5-27. Mutation.ts

```
import { Context } from '../index';
import { Post, Prisma } from '@prisma/client';

interface PostArgs {
    post: { title?: string; content?: string; }
}

interface PostPayloadType {
    userErrors: { message: string }[];
    post: Post | Prisma.Prisma__PostClient<Post> | null;
}
```

```
export const Mutation = {
    postCreate: async (_: any, { post }: PostArgs, { prisma }:
    Context): Promise<PostPayloadType> => {
        const { title, content } = post;
        if(!title || !content) {
            return { userErrors: [{ message: "You must provide
            title and content"}], post: null }
        }
        return {userErrors: [], post: prisma.post.create({
        data:{ title, content, authorId: 1 }})}
    },
}
```

Now, we will write the postUpdate mutation in the Mutation.ts
file. Here, we are first again checking if both the title and the content are
present. After that, we are finding the post with the findUnique method by
passing the ID.

If we are not able to find any post, we are returning a message. Lastly,
we are updating the specific post with the payload. See Listing 5-28.

Listing 5-28. Mutation.ts

```
postUpdate: async (_: any, { post, postId }: {postId:
string, post: PostArgs["post"]}, { prisma }: Context):
Promise<PostPayloadType> => {
    const { title, content } = post;
    if(!title && !content){
        return {
            userErrors: [{ message: "Atleast one field
            required"}],
            post: null
        }
    }
```

186

```
    const existingPost = await prisma.post.findUnique({
        where: { id: Number(postId)},
    });

    if (!existingPost) {
        return {
            userErrors: [{ message: "Post does not
            exist"}],
            post: null
        };
    }
    let payloadToUpdate = { title, content};
    if (!title) delete payloadToUpdate.title;
    if (!content) delete payloadToUpdate.content;

    return {
        userErrors: [],
        post: prisma.post.update({
            data: { ...payloadToUpdate },
            where: { id: Number(postId) },
        }),
    };
},
```

Now, in the `schema.ts` file, we will update the ID and input. See
Listing 5-29.

Listing 5-29. schema.ts

```
type Mutation{
        postCreate(post: PostInput!): PostPayload!
        postUpdate(postId: ID!, post: PostInput!):
        PostPayload!
}
```

Now, with the `postUpdate` mutation in the GraphQL server, we can update a post. See Figure 5-19.

Figure 5-19. *GraphQL*

Creating the postDelete and postSignup Mutations

We will now add the definitions of a `postDelete` mutation in the `schema.ts` file. See Listing 5-30.

Listing 5-30. schema.ts

```
type Mutation{
        postCreate(post: PostInput!): PostPayload!
        postUpdate(postId: ID!, post: PostInput!):
        PostPayload!
        postDelete(postId: ID!): PostPayload!
}
```

Now, we will create the `postDelete` mutation in the `Mutation.ts` file. Here again we are finding the post with the `findUnique` method by passing the ID. Next, we are using the `delete` method to delete the post. See Listing 5-31.

Listing 5-31. Mutation.ts

```
postDelete: async (_: any, { postId }: { postId: string },
{ prisma }: Context): Promise<PostPayloadType> => {
    const post = await prisma.post.findUnique({ where: {
    id: Number(postId)} });
    if (!post) {
        return { userErrors: [{ message: "Post does not
        exist" }], post: null };
    }
    await prisma.post.delete({
        where: {
            id: Number(postId),
        },
    });

    return { userErrors: [], post };
},
```

Now, with the `postDelete` mutation in the GraphQL server, we can delete a post. See Figure 5-20.

Figure 5-20. *GraphQL*

We will now add the definitions of a signup mutation in the schema.ts file. See Listing 5-32.

Listing 5-32. schema.ts

```
type Mutation{
        postCreate(post: PostInput!): PostPayload!
        postUpdate(postId: ID!, post: PostInput!):
        PostPayload!
        postDelete(postId: ID!): PostPayload!
        signup(email: String! , name: String!, password:
        String! bio: String!): User
}
```

Now, we will create the signup mutation in the Mutation.ts file. Here, we are just creating a user through the create method, by passing the email, name, and password. See Listing 5-33.

Listing 5-33. Mutation.ts

```
interface SignupArgs {
    email: string;
    name: string;
    password: string;
    bio: string;
}

export const Mutation = {
    signup: async (_: any, { email, name, password }:
    SignupArgs, { prisma }: Context) => {
        return prisma.user.create({ data: { email, name,
        password }})
    },
}
```

Now, with the `signup` mutation in the GraphQL server, we can create a new user. See Figure 5-21.

Figure 5-21. *GraphQL*

We can check the newly created user in Prisma Studio. See Figure 5-22.

Figure 5-22. *Studio*

Adding Validators

We will add validations in our project. So, first install the validator in our `server` folder.

Since we are using TypeScript, we also need to install the types for it. See Listing 5-34.

Listing 5-34. Terminal

```
npm i validator@13.6.0 @types/validator@13.6.4
```

Now, we will add AuthPayload as a return type in the schema.ts file. Here, we are giving userErrors as a required array and also the user, which is of type User. See Listing 5-35.

Listing 5-35. schema.ts

```
type Mutation{
        postDelete(postId: ID!): PostPayload!
        signup(email: String! , name: String!, password:
        String! bio: String!): AuthPayload!
}

type AuthPayload {
        userErrors: [UserError!]!
        user: User
}
```

Next, we will use the validators in the Mutation.ts file. We are also including a bio in the sign-up mutation. See Listing 5-36.

Listing 5-36. Mutation.ts

```
interface UserPayload {
    userErrors: { message: string }[];
    user: null;
}

export const Mutation = {
    signup: async (_: any, { email, name, password, bio }:
    SignupArgs, { prisma }: Context): Promise<UserPayload> => {
        const isEmail = validator.isEmail(email);
```

```
if (!isEmail) return { userErrors: [{ message: "Email
Invalid"}], user: null};
const isValidPassword = validator.isLength(password, {
min: 5 });
if (!isValidPassword) return { userErrors: [{ message:
"Minimum 5 length is required"}], user: null};
if (!name || !bio) return { userErrors: [{ message:
"Bio or name invalid"}], user: null};

return {userErrors: [], user: null }
// return prisma.user.create({ data: { email, name,
    password }})
    },
}
```

Now, if we give a wrong email in GraphQL Studio, we will get an error. See Figure 5-23.

Figure 5-23. *GraphQL*

Also, a shorter password will give an error. See Figure 5-24.

Figure 5-24. *GraphQL*

Password Encrypting

Our passwords are stored as plain text in the database, which is not a good thing. We will install the bcryptjs package in our server.

We will also install the types for it. See Listing 5-37.

Listing 5-37. Terminal

```
npm i bcryptjs@2.4.3 @types/bcryptjs@2.4.2
```

Now, in the Mutation.ts file, we will hash the password with bcrypt. hash(). And we are passing the hashed value, while creating a new user. See Listing 5-38.

194

Listing 5-38. Mutation.ts

```
import bcrypt from "bcryptjs";

export const Mutation = {
    signup: async (_: any, { email, name, password, bio }:
    SignupArgs, { prisma }: Context): Promise<UserPayload> => {
        if (!name || !bio) return { userErrors: [{ message:
        "Bio or name invalid"}], user: null};
        const hashedPassword = await bcrypt.hash(password, 10);
        await prisma.user.create({ data: { email, name,
        password: hashedPassword }} );
        return {userErrors: [], user: null }
    },
}
```

Now, when we create a new user, the password will be hashed. See Figure 5-25.

Figure 5-25. *Studio*

Implementing JWT

Now, we will implement JWT token in our project so that we don't have to log in again and again. First, we will change AuthPayload to have the token in the schema.ts file. See Listing 5-39.

Listing 5-39. schema.ts

```
type AuthPayload {
        userErrors: [UserError!]!
        token: String
}
```

Next, we will install jsonwebtoken and types of it in our project in the Mutation.ts file. See Listing 5-40.

Listing 5-40. Mutation.ts

```
import JWT from "jsonwebtoken";
import { JWT_SIGNATURE } from '../keys';

interface UserPayload {
    userErrors: { message: string }[];
    token: string | null;
}
```

We will do the necessary imports and also add a type for the token in the UserPayload interface. See Listing 5-41.

Listing 5-41. Terminal

```
npm i jsonwebtoken@8.5.1 @types/jsonwebtoken@8.5.5
```

In a keys.ts file, we will export the JWT_SIGNATURE with any random key. See Listing 5-42.

Listing 5-42. keys.ts

```
export const JWT_SIGNATURE="welcome2graphql"
```

We will add the .env and keys.ts files in the .gitignore file. See Listing 5-43.

Listing 5-43. .env

```
node_modules
.env
keys.ts
```

Now, in the Mutation.ts file, we will make the token null for invalid fields. We will use JWT to sign in with the user email and JWT_SIGNATURE. We will also give an expiry time in it. See Listing 5-44.

Listing 5-44. Mutation.ts

```
signup: async (_: any, { email, name, password, bio }:
SignupArgs, { prisma }: Context): Promise<UserPayload> => {
    const isEmail = validator.isEmail(email);
    if (!isEmail) return { userErrors: [{ message: "Email
    Invalid"}], token: null};
    const isValidPassword = validator.isLength(password, {
    min: 5 });
    if (!isValidPassword) return { userErrors: [{ message:
    "Minimum 5 length is required"}], token: null};
    if (!name || !bio) return { userErrors: [{ message:
    "Bio or name invalid"}], token: null};
    const hashedPassword = await bcrypt.hash(password, 10);
    const user = await prisma.user.create({ data: { email,
    name, password: hashedPassword }} );
    const token = await JWT.sign({ userId: user.id, email:
    user.email }, JWT_SIGNATURE, { expiresIn: 3600 });
    return {userErrors: [], token }
},
```

We will also create a profile in the Mutation.ts file. Besides that, we have refactored our code. See Listing 5-45.

197

Listing 5-45. Mutation.ts

```
signup: async (_: any, { email, name, password, bio }:
SignupArgs, { prisma }: Context): Promise<UserPayload> => {
    const hashedPassword = await bcrypt.hash(password, 10);
    const user = await prisma.user.create({ data: { email,
    name, password: hashedPassword }} );
    await prisma.profile.create({ data: { bio, userId:
    user.id }});
    return {userErrors: [], token: JWT.sign({ userId: user.
    id }, JWT_SIGNATURE, { expiresIn: 3600 })}
},
```

Now, we will see a `Profile` field in the Prisma sandbox. See
Figure 5-26.

Figure 5-26. *Studio*

Now, when we do the sign-up mutation, by passing all the required
fields, we will get the token back. See Figure 5-27.

Figure 5-27. *GraphQL*

We will also see in the Prisma sandbox that a user has been created with a profile. See Figure 5-28.

Figure 5-28. *Studio*

Creating the Sign-in Mutation

Now, we will create the sign-in mutation. First, we will add the input credentials in the sign-up definition in the schema.ts file. Next, we will create a sign-in definition with the credentials type. See Listing 5-46.

Listing 5-46. schema.ts

```
type Mutation{
    postCreate(post: PostInput!): PostPayload!
    postUpdate(postId: ID!, post: PostInput!): PostPayload!
    postDelete(postId: ID!): PostPayload!
    signup(credentials: CredentialsInput , name: String!,
    bio: String!): AuthPayload!
    signin(credentials: CredentialsInput): AuthPayload!
}

input CredentialsInput {
    email: String!
    password: String!
}
```

Next, we will update our interface for `SignupArgs` in the `Mutation.ts` file and use it. See Listing 5-47.

Listing 5-47. Mutation.ts

```
interface SignupArgs {
    credentials: {
            email: string;
            password: string;
    }
    name: string;
    bio: string;
}
```

```
export const Mutation = {
    signup: async (_: any, { credentials, name, bio }:
    SignupArgs, { prisma }: Context): Promise<UserPayload> => {
        const { email, password } = credentials;
        const isEmail = validator.isEmail(email);

    },
}
```

We will also create a new interface for `SigninArgs` in the `Mutation.ts` file.

Next, we will write the `signin` mutation in the `Mutation.ts` file. Here, we are first finding the unique user with the email. After that, we are using `bcrypt.compare` to compare the password with the stored password.

We are returning the token upon successfully logging in. See Listing 5-48.

Listing 5-48. Mutation.ts

```
interface SigninArgs {
    credentials: {
        email: string;
        password: string;
    };
}

export const Mutation = {
    signin: async (_: any, { credentials }: SigninArgs,
    { prisma }: Context): Promise<UserPayload> => {
        const { email, password } = credentials;
        const user = await prisma.user.findUnique({ where:
        { email } });
        if (!user) return { userErrors: [{ message: "Invalid
        credentials" }], token: null };
```

```
    const isMatch = await bcrypt.compare(password, user.
    password);

    if (!isMatch) return { userErrors: [{ message: "Invalid
    credentials" }], token: null };
    return {userErrors: [], token: JWT.sign({ userId:
    user.id }, JWT_SIGNATURE, { expiresIn: 3600 })}
  }
}
```

Now, in GraphQL Studio, when we sign in with the correct email and password, we will get the token back. See Figure 5-29.

Figure 5-29. *GraphQL*

Authorized User

We want only authorized users to create, update, or delete a post. So, we will first create an utils folder in the src folder. Inside it, we will create a file called getUser.ts and add the content shown in Listing 5-49 to it.

Here, we are using `JWT.verify()` to verify the use of the token and our secret.

Listing 5-49. getUser.ts

```
import JWT from "jsonwebtoken";
import { JWT_SIGNATURE } from "../keys";

export const getUser = (token: string) => {
    try {
        return JWT.verify(token, JWT_SIGNATURE) as { userId:
        number };
    } catch (error) {
        return null;
    }
};
```

Now, in the `index.ts` file, we will import `getUser` and create a `userInfo` context. We will call this `getUser` function with the token, which we will receive as authorization. See Listing 5-50.

Listing 5-50. index.ts

```
import { Mutation } from "./resolvers/Mutation";
import { getUser } from "./utils/getUser";

const prisma = new PrismaClient();

export interface Context {
    prisma: PrismaClient<
        Prisma.PrismaClientOptions,
        never,
        Prisma.RejectOnNotFound | Prisma.RejectPerOperation |
        undefined
    >;
```

```
    userInfo: { userId: number } | null;
}

const server = new ApolloServer({
    typeDefs,
    resolvers: {
        Query, Mutation
    },
    context: async ({ req }: any): Promise<Context> => {
        const userInfo = await getUser(req.headers.
        authorization);
        return { prisma, userInfo };
    },
})
```

Next, in the postCreate mutation in the Mutation.ts file, we will get the userInfo value. Here, we are returning if we are not getting the userInfo. If we get the value, we extract the userId value from it and assign it to the authorId. See Listing 5-51.

Listing 5-51. Mutation.ts

```
postCreate: async (_: any, { post }: PostArgs, { prisma,
userInfo }: Context): Promise<PostPayloadType> => {
    if (!userInfo) return { userErrors: [{ message:
    "Forbidden access (unauthenticated)"}], post: null };
    const { title, content } = post;
    if(!title || !content) {
        return { userErrors: [{ message: "You must provide
        title and content"}], post: null }
    }
    return {userErrors: [], post: prisma.post.create({
    data:{ title, content, authorId: userInfo.userId }})}
},
```

Now, if we just try to create a post, we will get the "Forbidden access" error in Apollo Studio. See Figure 5-30.

Figure 5-30. *GraphQL*

So, we will pass a token of a user for the authorization, and the post will be created. See Figure 5-31.

Figure 5-31. *GraphQL*

We want only the user who created the post to be able to update or delete it. So, we will create a userUpdatePost.ts file in the utils folder.

Here, we are finding the user and the post. The main thing that we are checking here is that the authorId of the post and the user ID are the same. See Listing 5-52.

Listing 5-52. userUpdatePost.ts

```
import { Context } from "..";

interface UserUpdatePostParams {
    userId: number;
    postId: number;
    prisma: Context["prisma"];
}
export const userUpdatePost = async ({ userId, postId, prisma
}: UserUpdatePostParams) => {
    const user = await prisma.user.findUnique({ where: { id:
    userId } });
    if(!user) return { userErrors: [{ message: "User not found"
    }], post: null };
    const post = await prisma.post.findUnique({ where: { id:
    postId }});
    if(post?.authorId !== user.id) return { userErrors: [{
    message: "Post not owned" }], post: null };
}
```

Now, we are calling the userUpdatePost function from the postUpdate mutation in the Mutation.ts file. If we get an error, we are returning from this function. See Listing 5-53.

Listing 5-53. Mutation.ts

```
import { userUpdatePost } from '../utils/userUpdatePost';

postUpdate: async (_: any, { post, postId }: {postId: string,
post: PostArgs["post"]}, { prisma, userInfo }: Context):
Promise<PostPayloadType> => {
    if (!userInfo) return { userErrors: [{ message: "Forbidden
    access (unauthenticated)"}], post: null };
    const error = await userUpdatePost({ userId: userInfo.
    userId, postId: Number(postId), prisma });
    if (error) return error;
    const { title, content } = post;
...
},
```

Now, we will also call the userUpdatePost function from the postDelete mutation in the Mutation.ts file. We have added the userInfo here. See Listing 5-54.

Listing 5-54. Mutation.ts

```
    postDelete: async (_: any, { postId }: { postId:
    string }, { prisma, userInfo }: Context):
    Promise<PostPayloadType> => {
        if (!userInfo) return { userErrors: [{ message:
        "Forbidden access (unauthenticated)"}], post: null };
        const error = await userUpdatePost({ userId: userInfo.
        userId, postId: Number(postId), prisma });
        if (error) return error;
        const post = await prisma.post.findUnique({ where: {
        id: Number(postId)} });
    ...
    },
```

Now, we have a post with an ID of 5 associated with the user Nabendu Biswas in our database. See Figure 5-32.

Figure 5-32. *Studio*

If we try to delete this post, we will get a forbidden error. See Figure 5-33.

Figure 5-33. *GraphQL*

But if we pass the token for Nabendu Biswas, we will be able to delete the post successfully. See Figure 5-34.

Figure 5-34. *GraphQL*

Publishing and Unpublishing Posts

A user can have a post in an unpublish state where only they can see it.
Everyone else can see the post only if it is published. We will write the
definitions of postPublish and postUnPublish in the schema.ts file. See
Listing 5-55.

Listing 5-55. schema.ts

```
type Mutation{
    postCreate(post: PostInput!): PostPayload!
    postUpdate(postId: ID!, post: PostInput!): PostPayload!
    postDelete(postId: ID!): PostPayload!
    postPublish(postId: ID!): PostPayload!
    postUnPublish(postId: ID!): PostPayload!
    signup(credentials: CredentialsInput , name: String!,
    bio: String!): AuthPayload!
    signin(credentials: CredentialsInput): AuthPayload!
}
```

Now, we will add the methods of postPublish and postUnPublish in the Mutation.ts file. Here in postPublish, we are first checking if the user has access to this post and, if they do, then setting published to true. In postUnPublish, we are doing the opposite and setting published to false. See Listing 5-56.

Listing 5-56. Mutation.ts

```
postPublish: async (_: any, { postId }: { postId:
string }, { prisma, userInfo }: Context):
Promise<PostPayloadType> => {
    if (!userInfo) return { userErrors: [{ message:
    "Forbidden access (unauthenticated)"}], post: null };
    const error = await userUpdatePost({ userId: userInfo.
    userId, postId: Number(postId), prisma });
    if (error) return error;
    return { userErrors: [], post: prisma.post.update({
        where: { id: Number(postId) },
        data: { published: true }
    })};
},
postUnPublish: async (_: any, { postId }: {
postId: string }, { prisma, userInfo }: Context):
Promise<PostPayloadType> => {
    if (!userInfo) return { userErrors: [{ message:
    "Forbidden access (unauthenticated)"}], post: null };
    const error = await userUpdatePost({ userId: userInfo.
    userId, postId: Number(postId), prisma });
    if (error) return error;
```

```
      return { userErrors: [], post: prisma.post.update({
         where: { id: Number(postId) },
            data: { published: false }
      })};
   },
```

Now, we have a post with `published` set to `false` in the database. See Figure 5-35.

Figure 5-35.   *Studio*

We can set `published` to `true` by giving the `postPublish` mutation with the correct token. See Figure 5-36.

Figure 5-36.   *GraphQL*

211

Other Queries

We will create three useful queries now. The first one is a me query, which will allow a user to see all of their information. First add the me query to the schema.ts file. See Listing 5-57.

Listing 5-57. schema.ts

```
export const typeDefs = gql`
    type Query {
        me: User
        posts: [Post!]!
    }
`
```

Now, we will write the code for it in the Query.ts file. Here, we are finding the user with the provided ID. See Listing 5-58.

Listing 5-58. Query.ts

```
export const Query = {
    me: (_: any, __: any, { userInfo, prisma }: Context) => {
        if (!userInfo) return null;
        return prisma.user.findUnique({
            where: { id: userInfo.userId },
        });
    },
    posts: (_: any, __: any, { prisma }: Context) => {
        ...
    },
}
```

Next, we will run the query in the GraphQL sandbox with the token, and we will get back the data. See Figure 5-37.

Figure 5-37. *GraphQL*

The next query we will make is the profile query, which can be used by any user to get the profile data of another user. So, we will first add it in the schema.ts file. See Listing 5-59.

Listing 5-59. schema.ts

```
type Query {
    me: User
    posts: [Post!]!
    profile(userId: ID!): Profile
}
```

Next, we will create the profile query in the Query.ts file. Here, we are returning the profile when passing the userId value. See Listing 5-60.

Listing 5-60. Query.ts

```
export const Query = {
    ...
    profile: async ( _: any, { userId }: { userId: string }, {
    prisma }: Context ) => {
        return prisma.profile.findUnique({ where: { userId:
        Number(userId) }});
    }
}
```

Now, we also need to create a Profile.ts file in the resolvers folder. Here, we are returning the user based on the ID. See Listing 5-61.

Listing 5-61. Profile.ts

```
import { Context } from "..";

interface ProfileParentType {
    id: number;
    bio: string;
    userId: number;
}

export const Profile = {
    user: (parent: ProfileParentType, __: any, { userInfo,
    prisma }: Context) => {
        return prisma.user.findUnique({ where: { id: parent.
        userId} });
    },
};
```

Now, we will add Profile to the resolvers in the index.ts file. See Listing 5-62.

Listing 5-62. index.ts

```
import { getUser } from "./utils/getUser";
import { Profile } from "./resolvers/Profile";

const prisma = new PrismaClient();

export interface Context {
    ...
}

const server = new ApolloServer({
    typeDefs,
    resolvers: {
        Query, Mutation, Profile
    },
    context: async ({ req }: any): Promise<Context> => {
        const userInfo = await getUser(req.headers.
        authorization);
        return { prisma, userInfo };
    },
})
```

Now, if we run a query for the profile, we will get the data back. See Figure 5-38.

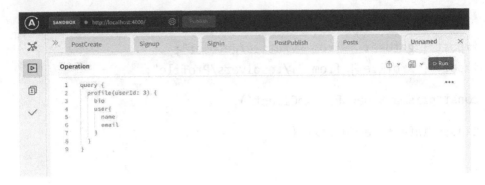

Figure 5-38. GraphQL

Lastly, we will update our Post query to showcase the user of a post. First, we will create a new Post.ts file inside the resolvers folder. Here, again we are finding the user from the authorId value of the parent. See Listing 5-63.

Listing 5-63. Post.ts

```
import { Context } from "..";

interface PostParentType {
    authorId: number;
}

export const Post = {
    user: (parent: PostParentType, __: any, { prisma }:
    Context) => {
        return prisma.user.findUnique({ where: { id: parent.
        authorId }});
    },
};
```

Next, we will add Post in the resolvers in the index.ts file. See Listing 5-64.

Listing 5-64. index.ts

```
import { Post } from "./resolvers/Post";

const prisma = new PrismaClient();

const server = new ApolloServer({
    typeDefs,
    resolvers: {
        Query, Mutation, Profile, Post
    },
})
```

Now, we need to create a User.ts file in the resolvers folder. Here, we are first checking whether the user is searching for their own profile and then return all posts that belong to them . If the user is different, then we send only the published posts. See Listing 5-65.

Listing 5-65. User.ts

```
import { Context } from "..";

interface UserParentType {
    id: number;
}

export const User = {
    posts: (parent: UserParentType, __: any, { userInfo, prisma
}: Context) => {
        const isOwnProfile = parent.id === userInfo?.userId;
        if (isOwnProfile) {
            return prisma.post.findMany({ where: { authorId:
            parent.id }, orderBy: [{createdAt: "desc"}]});
        } else {
```

217

```
        return prisma.post.findMany({where: {authorId:
        parent.id, published: true}, orderBy:
            [{ createdAt: "desc" }]});
    }
  },
};
```

Now, we will update the posts in Query.ts to show only the published posts. See Listing 5-66.

Listing 5-66. Query.ts

```
posts: (_: any, __: any, { prisma }: Context) => {
    return prisma.post.findMany({
        where: { published: true },
        orderBy: [{ createdAt: "desc" }]
    });
},
```

Finally, we will add the user in the index.ts file. See Listing 5-67.

Listing 5-67. index.ts

```
import { User } from "./resolvers/User";

const prisma = new PrismaClient();

const server = new ApolloServer({
    typeDefs,
    resolvers: {
        Query, Mutation, Profile, Post, User
    },
    ...
})
```

Now, when we query a profile by passing a userId value, we will get all the data and published posts back. This user has no published posts. See Figure 5-39.

Figure 5-39.   *GraphQL*

If we pass the token of the user, we will get unpublished posts also. See Figure 5-40.

Figure 5-40.   *GraphQL*

Summary

In this chapter, we created a back-end app with Prisma. We configured Prisma and created various queries and mutations. We also added password encryption and implemented JWT. Now that our back end is completed, we will create the front end of this app in the next chapter.

CHAPTER 6

Connecting with the Front End

In this chapter, we will connect the front end to the backend of the blog app that we created in the previous chapter.

The Setup

In the directory of `blog-app-prisma`, we will add a `client` folder containing our basic React app. We will start with the initial code, which can be found at https://drive.google.com/file/d/1xx6T7tWk5SOSfg5FE6hKx_QXJ6IaZv8p/view?usp=sharing.

Here, in the `App.js` file, we have different routes showing different components. See Listing 6-1.

Listing 6-1. App.js

```
import "./App.css";
import { Route, Switch } from "react-router";
import Posts from "./pages/Posts/Posts";
import Profile from "./pages/Profile/Profile";
import "bootstrap/dist/css/bootstrap.min.css";
import Signup from "./pages/Signup/Signup";
import Signin from "./pages/Signin/Signin";
```

© Nabendu Biswas 2023
N. Biswas, *Practical GraphQL*, https://doi.org/10.1007/978-1-4842-9621-9_6

```
function App() {
  return (
    <div className="App">
      <Switch>
        <Route strict exact path="/" component={Posts} />
        <Route strict path="/signup" component={Signup} />
        <Route strict path="/signin" component={Signin} />
        <Route strict path="/profile/:id"
        component={Profile} />
      </Switch>
    </div>
  );
}

export default App;
```

After installing the required packages with `npm install` and starting the app with `npm start`, we can go to a route and see the component. See Figure 6-1.

Figure 6-1. *Localhost*

Connecting the Client to the Server and the First Query

Now, we will connect our client to the server using the Apollo client. So, inside the `client` folder, we need to install the packages `@apollo/client` and `graphql`. See Listing 6-2.

Listing 6-2. Terminal

```
cd client
npm i @apollo/client@3.6.9 graphql@15.8.0
```

In the `index.js` file, we will create an instance of `ApolloClient` and pass the URL for our server, along with the required configuration of cache. Next, we will wrap the whole app with `ApolloProvider` and pass this client. See Listing 6-3.

Listing 6-3. index.js

```
import React from "react";
import ReactDOM from "react-dom";
import "./index.css";
import App from "./App";
import { BrowserRouter } from "react-router-dom";
import { ApolloProvider, ApolloClient, InMemoryCache } from "@
apollo/client";

const client = new ApolloClient({
  uri: "http://localhost:4000/graphql",
  cache: new InMemoryCache()
})
```

```
ReactDOM.render(
  <React.StrictMode>
    <BrowserRouter>
    <ApolloProvider client={client}>
      <App />
    </ApolloProvider>
    </BrowserRouter>
  </React.StrictMode>,
  document.getElementById("root")
);
```

Now, in the Posts.js file, we will import gql from the Apollo client. After that, we will create the variable GET_POSTS, which will contain our query to get all the posts and different fields in it. This is the same query we used in Apollo Studio in the previous chapter.

Next, in the Posts function in the Posts.js file, we will extract the data, error, and loading info from our query by using useQuery and passing GET_POSTS in it. After that, we loop through the array of posts by using a map and passing each post to a Post component. See Listing 6-4.

Listing 6-4. Posts.js

```
import React from "react";
import Post from "../../components/Post/Post";
import { gql, useQuery } from "@apollo/client";

const GET_POSTS = gql`
  query {
    posts {
      id
      title
      content
      createdAt
```

```
      user{
        name
      }
    }
  }
`
```

```
export default function Posts() {
  const { data, error, loading } = useQuery(GET_POSTS);
  if(error) return <h1>Error Page</h1>
  if(loading) return <h1>Loading...</h1>
  const { posts } = data;

  return <div>
    {posts.map(post => (
      <Post key={post.id} title={post.title} content={post.
      content} date={post.createdAt} id={post.id} user={post.
      user.name}
      />))}
  </div>;
}
```

In the Post.js file, we are simply taking all the props and showing them. See Listing 6-5.

Listing 6-5. Post.js

```
import "./Post.css";

const Post = ({ title, content, date, user, published,
id }) => {
  const formatedDate = new Date(Number(date));

  return (
    <div className="post">
```

225

```
      <div className="post__header">
        <h3>{title}</h3>
        <h4>Created At {`${formatedDate}`.split(" ").splice
        (0, 3).join(" ")} by{" "}{user}</h4>
      </div>
      <p>{content}</p>
    </div>
  )
}
export default Post
```

We have also put some basic styles into our Post component in the
Post.css file. See Listing 6-6.

Listing 6-6. Post.css

```
.post {
  background-color: rgb(193, 215, 235);
  margin-bottom: 1rem;
  padding: 1rem;
}

.post__header{
  display: flex;
  align-items: center;
  justify-content: space-between;
}

.post__header h4 {
  font-size: 0.8rem;
}
```

Now, at http://localhost:3000, we will see all of our posts. See
Figure 6-2.

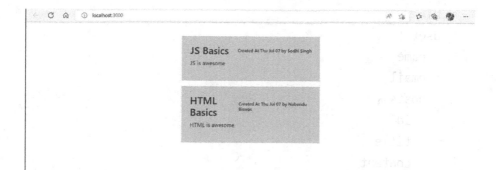

Figure 6-2. *Localhost*

Querying with Variables

In the Profile.js file, the variable GET_PROFILE will contain our query to get the profile; we do this by passing the userId variable.

We pass the variable userId in useQuery in the Profile.js file. Now, we are getting this from the useParams() hook, which takes it from the address bar.

The username and bio are returned. See Listing 6-7.

Listing 6-7. Profile.js

```
import React from "react";
import { useParams } from "react-router";
import AddPostModal from "../../components/AddPostModal/
AddPostModal";
import Post from "../../components/Post/Post";
import { gql, useQuery } from "@apollo/client";

const GET_PROFILE = gql`
  query GetProfile($userId: ID!){
    profile(userId: $userId) {
      id
```

```
      bio
      user {
        name
        email
        posts {
          id
          title
          content
          createdAt
        }
      }
    }
  }
}


export default function Profile() {
  const { id } = useParams();
  const { data, error, loading } = useQuery(GET_PROFILE, {
  variables: { userId: id } });
  if(error) return <h1>Error Page</h1>
  if(loading) return <h1>Loading...</h1>
  const { profile } = data;

  return (
    <div>
      <div style={{ marginBottom: "2rem", display: "flex ",
      justifyContent: "space-between" }}>
        <div>
          <h1>{profile.user.name}</h1>
          <p>{profile.bio}</p>
        </div>
        <div>{"profile" ? <AddPostModal /> : null}</div>
```

```
      </div>
      <div></div>
    </div>
  );
}
```

Now, if we go to a valid profile such as 7, as in `http://localhost:3000/profile/7`, we will get the details of the user. See Figure 6-3.

Figure 6-3. *Localhost*

We will also show the post of this profile. So, we will map through the posts and pass individual post to the `Post` component. See Listing 6-8.

Listing 6-8. Profile.js

```
return (
  <div>
    <div style={{ marginBottom: "2rem", display: "flex ",
    justifyContent: "space-between" }}>
      <div>
        <h1>{profile.user.name}</h1>
        <p>{profile.bio}</p>
      </div>
      <div>{"profile" ? <AddPostModal /> : null}</div>
    </div>
    <div>
      {profile.user.posts.map(post =>
        <Post
```

229

```
            key={post.id}
            title={post.title}
            content={post.content}
            date={post.createdAt}
            id={post.id}
            user={profile.user.name}
        />)}
    </div>
  </div>
);
```

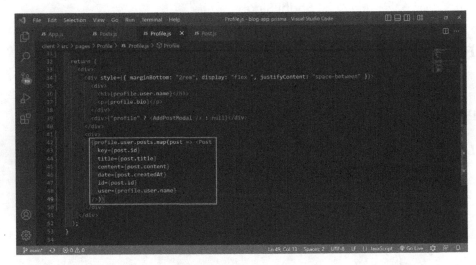

Figure 6-4. *Localhost and number*

Now, we will also get all the posts for this profile in localhost, as shown in Figure 6-5.

Figure 6-5. *Localhost*

Rendering Based on the User Profile

Now, we want to show the Add Post button only if the profile belongs to the user. We need to add a new field called isMyProfile in the schema.ts file of the server. See Listing 6-9.

Listing 6-9. schema.ts

```
type Profile {
    id: ID!
    bio: String!
    isMyProfile: Boolean!
    user: User!
}
```

Next, we will update the profile query in the Query.ts file. Here, we are checking if the passed-in userId is equal to userInfo.userID. We are returning the profile along with the isMyProfile variable. See Listing 6-10.

Listing 6-10. Query.ts

```
profile: async ( _: any, { userId }: { userId: string },
{ prisma, userInfo }: Context ) => {
    const isMyProfile = Number(userId) === userInfo?.userId
```

```
        const profile = await prisma.profile.findUnique({
        where: { userId: Number(userId) }});
        if(!profile) return null;
        return { ...profile, isMyProfile }
    }
```

Let's gack to our client. We will add an isMyProfile field in our GET_
PROFILE query inside the Profile.js file.

Now, in the return part of the Profile.js file, we will show the
AddPost- Modal component only if isMyProfile is true. See Listing 6-11.

Listing 6-11. Profile.ts

```
import { gql, useQuery } from "@apollo/client";

const GET_PROFILE = gql`
  query GetProfile($userId: ID!){
    profile(userId: $userId) {
      id
      bio
      isMyProfile
      user {
        name
        email
        posts {
          id
          title
          content
          createdAt
        }
      }
    }
  }
`
```

```
export default function Profile() {
  return (
    <div>
      <div style={{ marginBottom: "2rem", display: "flex ",
      justifyContent: "space-between" }}>
        <div>
          <h1>{profile.user.name}</h1>
          <p>{profile.bio}</p>
        </div>
        <div>{profile.isMyProfile ? <AddPostModal /> : null}
        </div>
      </div>
    </div>
  );
}
```

Since we have not implemented the authenticated logic yet, we will not see the Add Post button in any profile. See Figure 6-6.

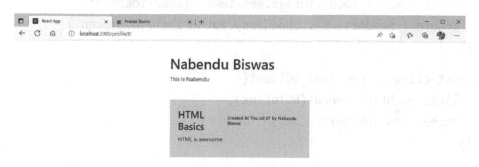

Figure 6-6. *Localhost*

Adding an Auth Token

Now, we will add an auth token in our front end so that it can be used to verify the user. In the index.js file, we are updating our header to take a token stored in the local storage with the name prisma- token. See Listing 6-12.

Listing 6-12. index.js

```
import { BrowserRouter } from "react-router-dom";
import { ApolloProvider, ApolloClient, InMemoryCache,
createHttpLink } from "@apollo/client";
import { setContext } from "@apollo/client/link/context";

const httpLink = createHttpLink({
  uri: "http://localhost:4000/graphql"
})

const authLink = setContext((_, { headers }) => {
  const token = localStorage.getItem("prisma-token");
  return { headers: { ...headers, authorization: token }}
})

const client = new ApolloClient({
  link: authLink.concat(httpLink),
  cache: new InMemoryCache()
})
```

Now, we will generate a token for a user with the mutation OS sign-in from Apollo Studio. See Figure 6-7.

Figure 6-7. *Studio*

Now, we will manually add this token in our local storage with the name prisma-token. See Figure 6-8.

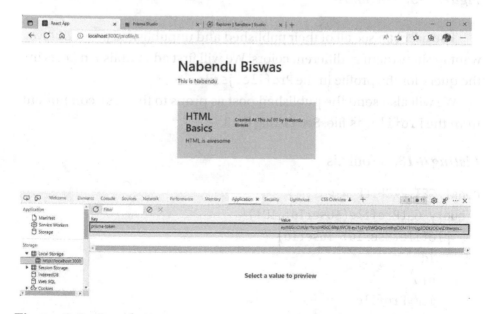

Figure 6-8. *Local storage*

Now, if we go to the profile for the user, whose token we are using, we will be able to see the Add Post button. See Figure 6-9.

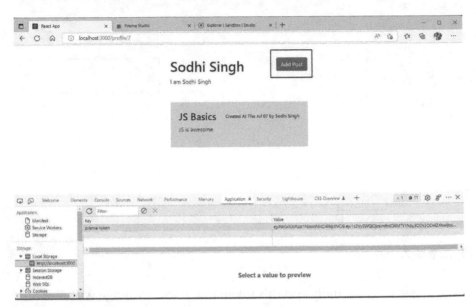

Figure 6-9. *Localhost*

The user can see all of their published and unpublished posts. But we want to show them in different colors. We will first add published posts in the query for the profile in the `Profile.js` file.

We will also send the published post as props to the `Post` component from the `Profile.js` file. See Listing 6-13.

Listing 6-13. Profile.js

```
const GET_PROFILE = gql`
  query GetProfile($userId: ID!){
    profile(userId: $userId) {
      id
      bio
      isMyProfile
```

```
      user {
        name
        email
        posts {
          id
          title
          content
          createdAt
          published
        }
      }
    }
  }
`

export default function Profile() {
  return (
    <div>
      <div>
        {profile.user.posts.map(post =>
          <Post
            key={post.id}
            title={post.title}
            content={post.content}
            date={post.createdAt}
            id={post.id}
            user={profile.user.name}
            published={post.published}
          />)}
      </div>
    </div>
  );
}
```

In the Post.js file, we will show the unpublished posts with a yellow background. See Listing 6-14.

Listing 6-14. Post.js

```
return (
  <div className="post" style={published === false ?
  { backgroundColor: 'yellow' }: {}}>
    <div className="post__header">
      <h3>{title}</h3>
      <h4>Created At {`${formatedDate}`.split(" ").splice
      (0, 3).join(" ")} by{" "}{user}</h4>
    </div>
    <p>{content}</p>
  </div>
)
```

Now, in the localhost, we will see the unpublished posts with a yellow background. See Figure 6-10.

Figure 6-10. *Localhost*

Next, we will also show Publish and Unpublish buttons for the logged-in user. So, we are sending the props of isMyProfile from the Profile.js file to the Post component. See Listing 6-15.

Listing 6-15. Profile.js

```
<div>
  {profile.user.posts.map(post =>
    <Post
      key={post.id}
      title={post.title}
      content={post.content}
      date={post.createdAt}
      id={post.id}
      user={profile.user.name}
      published={post.published}
      isMyProfile={profile.isMyProfile}
    />)}
</div>
```

Now, in the Post.js file, we will get the props of isMyProfile and use it will show a Publish or Unpublish button. See Listing 6-16.

Listing 6-16. Post.js

```
const Post = ({ title, content, date, user, published,
isMyProfile }) => {
  const formatedDate = new Date(Number(date));

  return (
    <div className="post" style={published === false ?
    { backgroundColor: 'yellow' }: {}}>
      {isMyProfile && published === false && <button
      className="post__btn">Publish</button>}
```

```
{isMyProfile && published && <button className="post__
btn">Unpublish</button>}
<div className="post__header">
  <h3>{title}</h3>
  <h4>Created At {`${formatedDate}`.split(" ").splice
  (0, 3).join(" ")} by{" "}{user}</h4>
</div>
<p>{content}</p>
</div>
)
}
```

We are also adding some CSS in the Post.css file for the button. See
Listing 6-17.

Listing 6-17. Post.css

```css
.post__btn{
  padding: 4px 6px;
  font-size: 0.6rem;
  text-transform: uppercase;
  border: none;
  background-color: darkblue;
  color: white;
  border-radius: 5px;
}

.post__btn:hover{
  cursor: pointer;
  background-color: darkmagenta;
}
```

Now, we will see some nice buttons for the logged-in user in localhost.
See Figure 6-11.

Figure 6-11. *Localhost*

The non-logged-in user will see only the published posts from the other user's profile. See Figure 6-12.

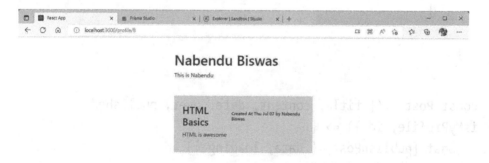

Figure 6-12. *Localhost*

Publishing and Unpublishing Mutations

Now, we will create the Publish and Unpublish mutations, which will add functionalities to the buttons created in the previous section.

So, in the `Post.js` file, first add the `PublishPost` mutation, which will take a `postId` value and return an error message and title. Now, to use it, we will use the `useMutation` hook from the Apollo client.

Lastly, the onClick of the Publish button will call the publishPost function. See Listing 6-18.

Listing 6-18. Post.js

```
import "./Post.css";
import { gql, useMutation } from "@apollo/client";

const PUBLISH_POST = gql`
  mutation PublishPost($postId: ID!) {
    postPublish(postId: $postId){
      userErrors{
        message
      }
      post {
        title
      }
    }
  }
`

const Post = ({ title, content, date, user, published,
isMyProfile, id }) => {
  const [publishPost, { data, loading }] =
  useMutation(PUBLISH_POST);
  const formatedDate = new Date(Number(date));
  return (
    <div className="post" style={published === false ? {
    backgroundColor: 'yellow' }: {}}>
      {isMyProfile && published === false && <button
      onClick={() => publishPost({ variables: { postId: id }})}
      className="post__btn">Publish</button>}
```

```
{isMyProfile && published && <button className="post__
btn">Unpublish</button>}
<div className="post__header">
</div>
    </div>
  )
}

export default Post
```

Now, we have clicked the first post, and it has become Published in the localhost. See Figure 6-13.

Figure 6-13. *Localhost*

We will create another mutation for UnPublishPost in the Post.js file. The logic will be same as the Publish post, and we will attach it to the onClick of the Unpublish button. See Listing 6-19.

Listing 6-19. Post.js

```
const UNPUBLISH_POST = gql`
  mutation UnPublishPost($postId: ID!) {
    postUnPublish(postId: $postId){
      userErrors{
        message
      }
      post {
        title
      }
    }
  }
`

const Post = ({ title, content, date, user, published,
isMyProfile, id }) => {
  const [publishPost, { data, loading }] = useMutation
  (PUBLISH_POST);
  const [unPublishPost, { data: unData, loading: unLoading }] =
  useMutation(UNPUBLISH_POST);
  const formatedDate = new Date(Number(date));

  return (
    <div className="post" style={published === false ? {
    backgroundColor: 'yellow' } : {}}>
      {isMyProfile && published === false && <button
      onClick={() => publishPost({ variables: { postId: id }
      })} className="post__btn">Publish</button>}
      {isMyProfile && published && <button onClick={()
      => unPublishPost({ variables: { postId: id } })}
      className="post__btn">Unpublish</button>}
      <div className="post__header">
```

```
      <h3>{title}</h3>
      <h4>Created At {`${formatedDate}`.split(" ").splice
      (0, 3).join(" ")} by{" "}{user}</h4>
    </div>
    <p>{content}</p>
  </div>
);
}
```

Next, in localhost, we have clicked the Unpublish button to unpublish a post. See Figure 6-14.

Figure 6-14. *Localhost*

Creating the SignIn and SignUp Mutations

Now, we will add the logic of signing up and signing in to our app. So, in the Signin.js file, we will create a SignIn mutation, which will take a password and an email address and return an error message and token.

We are again using sigin mutation with the useMutation hook. Lastly, we are calling the sign-in function from handleClick. See Listing 6-20.

Listing 6-20. Signin.js

```
import Button from "@restart/ui/esm/Button";
import { gql, useMutation } from "@apollo/client";

const SIGNIN = gql`
  mutation SignIn($email: String!, $password: String!){
    signin(credentials: { password: $password, email:
    $email}) {
      userErrors {
        message
      }
      token
    }
  }
`

export default function Signin() {
  const [signin, { data, loading}] = useMutation(SIGNIN);
  const [email, setEmail] = useState("");
  const [password, setPassword] = useState("");
  console.log(data);
  const handleClick = () => {
    signin({ variables: { email, password}})
  };
```

Now, in a browser, visit http://localhost:3000/signin, enter the wrong credentials, and click the SignIn button. In the console, we can see the userError for the invalid credentials. See Figure 6-15.

Figure 6-15. *Localhost*

Next, in the `Signin.js` file, we will create the `state` variable of the message inside an `useEffect`, which will be fired whenever we update the data. Here, we are first checking if there is an error and setting it through `setMessage`.

If we don't have an error and get back the token, we are setting it in the local storage of the `prisma-token` variable.

Finally, inside the response, we are showing the message if it is received. See Listing 6-21.

Listing 6-21. Signin.js

```
const [message, setMessage] = useState(null);
useEffect(() => {
  if(data && data.signin.userErrors.length) setMessage
  (data.signin.userErrors[0].message);
  if(data && data.signin.token) {
```

```
      localStorage.setItem("prisma-token", data.signin.token);
      setMessage('SignIn successfully. Token Saved');
    }
  },[data])

  return (
    <div>
      <Form>
        <Form.Group className="mb-3">
        </Form.Group>
        <Form.Group className="mb-3">
        </Form.Group>

        {message && <p style={{ backgroundColor: 'blue', color:
        'white', padding: '5px'}}>{message}</p>}
        <Button onClick={handleClick}>Signin</Button>
      </Form>
    </div>
  );
}
```

Again, we will enter the wrong credentials to get a message showing the invalid credentials. See Figure 6-16.

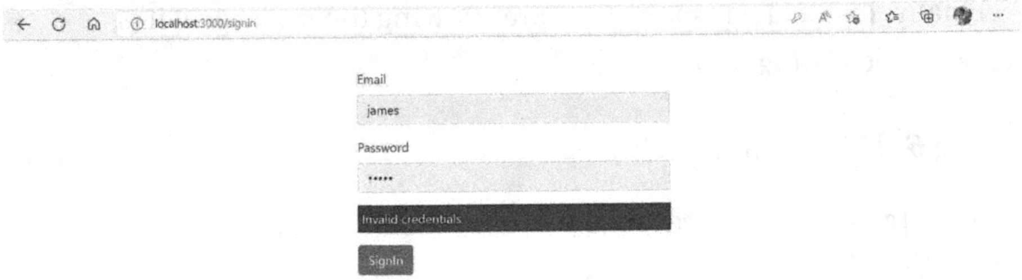

Figure 6-16. *Localhost*

But, if we give the correct credentials, we will get the sign-in successful message. Also, the `prisma-token` will get stored in local storage. See Figure 6-17.

Figure 6-17. *Localhost*

Now, in the `Signup.js` file, we will create a `SignUp` mutation, which will take a password, name, bio, and email and return an error message and token.

Again, we are using the same logic with `useEffect`, as shown in the `Signin.js` file. See Listing 6-22.

Listing 6-22. Signup.js

```
import { Form } from "react-bootstrap";
import { gql, useMutation } from "@apollo/client";

const SIGNUP = gql`
```

```
  mutation SignUp($email: String!, $password: String!, $name:
  String!, $bio: String!){
    signup(credentials: { password: $password, email: $email},
    name: $name, bio: $bio) {
      userErrors { message }
      token
    }
  }
```

```
export default function Signup() {
const [signup, { data, loading}] = useMutation(SIGNUP);

  const handleClick = () => signup({ variables: { email,
  password, name, bio}});
  const [message, setMessage] = useState(null);
  useEffect(() => {
    if(data && data.signup.userErrors.length) setMessage(data.
    signup.userErrors[0].message);
    if(data && data.signup.token) {
      localStorage.setItem("prisma-token", data.signup.token);
      setMessage('Signup successfully. Token Saved');
    }
  },[data])

  return (
    <div>
      <Form>
        <Form.Group className="mb-3">
        </Form.Group>
        <Form.Group className="mb-3">
        </Form.Group>
        <Form.Group className="mb-3">
        </Form.Group>
```

250

```
<Form.Group className="mb-3" controlId="exampleForm.
ControlTextarea1">
</Form.Group>
{message && <p style={{ backgroundColor: 'blue', color:
'white', padding: '5px'}}>{message}</p>}
<Button onClick={handleClick}>Signup</Button>
    </Form>
  </div>
);
}
```

Now, in a browser, visit http://localhost:3000/signup, enter the wrong email, and click the Signup button. We will see the message "Email Invalid." See Figure 6-18.

Figure 6-18. *Localhost*

If we enter everything correctly, we will see the sign-up successful message. See Figure 6-19.

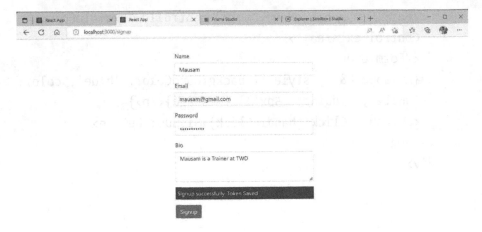

Figure 6-19. *Localhost*

We can also see in the database that a new user has been created. See Figure 6-20.

Figure 6-20. *Database*

Adding a Post Mutation

Now, in our AddPostModal.js file, we will add the PostCreate mutation. Here, we are providing the title and content and receiving the useErrors and post details.

We are also using this mutation with the useMutation hook.

Next, in the AddPostModal.js file, we will add the createPost call in handleClick. Here, we are also closing the modal. The message logic is the same as earlier. See Listing 6-23.

Listing 6-23. AddPostModal.js

```
import { gql, useMutation } from "@apollo/client";

const CREATE_POST = gql`
  mutation PostCreate($title: String!, $content: String!) {
    postCreate(post: { title: $title, content: $content }) {
      userErrors {
        message
      }
      post {
        title
        content
        published
        createdAt
        user {
          name
        }
      }
    }
  }
`

export default function AddPostModal() {
  const [createPost, { data, loading}] = useMutation
  (CREATE_POST);
  const [show, setShow] = useState(false);
  const handleClose = () => setShow(false);
  const handleShow = () => setShow(true);
  const [content, setContent] = useState("");
  const [title, setTitle] = useState("");
```

```
const handleClick = () => {
  createPost({ variables: { title, content }});
  handleClose();
};
const [message, setMessage] = useState(null);
useEffect(() => {
  if(data && data.postCreate.userErrors.length)
  setMessage(data.postCreate.userErrors[0].message);
},[data])

return (
  <>
    <Button variant="primary" onClick={handleShow}>
      Add Post
    </Button>

    <Modal
      show={show}
      onHide={handleClose}
      backdrop="static"
      keyboard={false}
    >
      <Modal.Header closeButton>
        <Modal.Title>Add Post</Modal.Title>
      </Modal.Header>
      <Modal.Body>
      {message && <p style={{ backgroundColor: 'blue',
      color: 'white', padding: '5px'}}>{message}</p>}
        <Form>
        ...
        </Form>
      </Modal.Body>
      ...
```

```
      </Modal.Footer>
    </Modal>
  </>
 );
}
```

Now, when we click the Add Post button, we will see a pop-up. Here, we will give a title and content and click the Add button. See Figure 6-21.

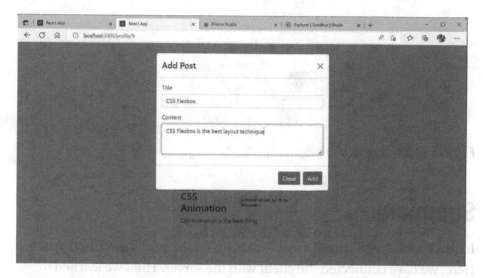

Figure 6-21. *Localhost*

We will be able to see the newly added post in our profile. See Figure 6-22.

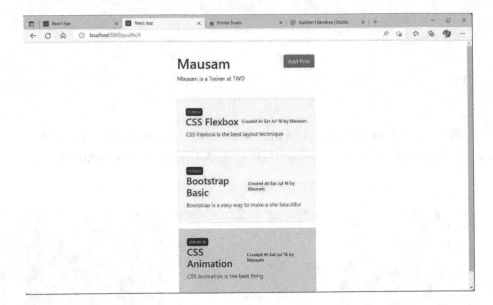

Figure 6-22. Localhost

Summary

In this chapter, we created a front-end app for the prima back-end app. Here, we have connected the client with the server. Then we learned to add an auth token and create `Publish` and `Unpublish` mutations. Also, you learned to create `Signin`, `Signup`, and `Post` mutations.

This completes the book. You can find the code for the entire blog app at `https://github.com/nabendu82/blog-app-prisma`.

Index

A

addClient mutation,
105, 107, 131–133
addProject mutation, 107, 110, 149
AddProject.js file, 144, 149
ADD_PROJECT
mutation, 148
APIs, 1, 3, 48
App.js file, 116, 119, 124, 125, 130,
136, 137, 221
Array of objects
allCourses, 19
resolvers, 20, 21
sandbox, 21
typeDefs, 20, 21
Array types
array of string, 15, 16, 19
error, 17, 18
not null, 17
null, 16, 18
Auth token
isMyProfile
logged-in user, 240, 241
non-logged-in user, 241
Post.css file, 240
Post.js file, 239, 240
Profile.js file, 239

prisma-token
Add Post button, 236
Apollo Studio, 234, 235
index.js file, 234
local storage, 235
Post.js file, 238
posts, 236, 238
Profile.js file, 236, 237
Average ratings
Query.js file, 47
schema.js file, 46
studio, 48

B

bcrypt.hash(), 194
blog-app-prisma, 163

C

Client to server
GET_POSTS, 224
index.js file, 223, 224
packages, 223
Post.css file, 226
posts, 226, 227
Posts.js file, 224–226
useQuery, 224

Printed in the United States
by Baker & Taylor Publisher Services